The Journey Towards Humility

The Journey Towards Humility

Self-Awareness

BRIAN LESLIE BISHOP

Foreword by Chris Deacy

RESOURCE *Publications* • Eugene, Oregon

THE JOURNEY TOWARDS HUMILITY
Self-Awareness

Resource Publications
An Imprint of Wipf and Stock Publishers
199 W. 8th Ave., Suite 3
Eugene, OR 97401

www.wipfandstock.com

PAPERBACK ISBN: 979-8-3852-6697-5
HARDCOVER ISBN: 979-8-3852-6698-2
EBOOK ISBN: 979-8-3852-6699-9

VERSION NUMBER 03/18/26

Foreword

In these pages, Brian Bishop offers more than just insight—he offers perspective shaped by a life of teaching, reflection and deep moral enquiry. His journey, from the classrooms of the east of England, to the wider terrain of literature, faith and philosophy reveals a man who has spent a lifetime asking not just what we know, but who we are.

This is a book grounded in *humility* not the meek mind, but the radical, searching *humility* of those who have truly looked at life. Brian draws on a rich tradition, from Chaucer's pilgrims to Francis of Assis's "holy fool," from Shakespeare's and Dostoevsky's tragic and haunted souls to the lucid anguish of Camus. These voices speak across centuries because they recognise what we still struggle to face: the limits of reason, the inevitability of suffering and the urgent need for compassion.

Brian writes, too, under the long shadow of the Holocaust, a reminder of how far we can fall when *humility* is lost. And yet he balances that darkness with light—in the simple, courageous faith of St. Francis, in the moral clarity of the holy fool, and in the quiet dignity of Jimmy Carter, whose Christian witness did not end in power, but in service.

Brian's work does not promise easy answers, what it offers instead is something rarer, a sense of accompaniment in a fractured world, he walks with the reader—gently, thoughtfully, towards deeper questions and toward a more honest kind of hope.

To read this book is to enter a conversation with a wise teacher and compassionate soul.

DR. CHRIS DEACY
Canterbury, Kent
June 30, 2025

Preface

THIS BOOK SEEKS TO consider the "HIDDEN CURRICULUM." This is an often used yet very difficult to define classification. It seems to have deteriorated into meaningless jargon. This has resulted, so it seems to me, in a debilitating void particularly in the education of our children.

As teachers of the younger generation which all the older generation are whether that is by profession, or as a simple fact of life, the social and moral lessons conveyed by who and what we are as human beings are automatically incorporated into our lessons. This fact should result in our profound HUMILITY. I hope that my writing helps to develop this understanding.

All references are to real people but their names and identities are not used unless prefaced with an "R" where their real names are appropriate.

To be, or not to be: that is the question:
Whether 'tis nobler in the mind to suffer
The slings and arrows of outrageous fortune,
Or to take arms against a sea of troubles,
And by opposing end them?

—SHAKESPEARE, *HAMLET*, ACT 3, SCENE 1

MAYBE HAMLET'S CONUNDRUM IS not the initial human awakening. However, wondering who or what one is, is a very early puzzle. This puzzle is never allowed to exercise us: answers arrive before that event. Our early schooling from parents and provisional teachers surrounds us as soon as we open our eyes. A confrontation with a doctor whom I was consulting when I was in the initial stages of my teaching career is rather noteworthy. This was in the UK in 1968. Going into a classroom is to be bombarded with minor ailments to which I had succumbed on a monthly basis. After a year of this, I asked the doctor if he could recommend how I might build a resistance to these infections. His reply which I quote verbatim remains with me. "Oh, what do I know? We doctors think we know a lot but we know very little. Take the liver, that vast chemical laboratory of the body and what do we know of it? Nothing. I had a heart attack recently and I gave up eating potatoes. I noticed I had fewer colds. You could try giving up potatoes."

I should state something that is probably obvious. The doctor was in the final stages of his journey as a doctor. I was beginning my journey as a professional teacher. Prior to that, of course, was my professional education at a school in the East End of London. On my first day in 1950, I was rounded up by a gang of villainous-looking east-enders who encircled me menacingly.

"Are you a Yid?"

I had no idea what a Yid was but I gathered the distinct impression that it was not a good idea to be one.

"You must be joking, Mate!"

I was released.

Prior to National Service, the Motor Manager of the insurance company that was employing me warned, "I do not want you back here after National Service, Bishop." A friend of mine at RAF Aldergrove who was demobbed before me lived in Bath. I visited. Bath was like coming up for air. I decamped to Bath and got a job with the Bath Co-operative Society. That summer I moved from Bath to the Lake District where I worked as an assistant warden at Holly How Youth Hostel, Coniston. I then joined the United Nations Association with a view to moving to Austria the following spring where along with drop-outs, conscientious objectors, and students I was to help build homes for refugees from Tito's Yugoslavia. My group was on loan to the Ockenden Venture in Haselmere, Surrey where a school was being established for displaced Polish children. We were general maintenance and labour for the autumn and winter of 1960. And then off to Austria for the spring and early summer of 1961. My father communicated through my mother that he was very disappointed in me: I was displaying all the signs of being work-shy. Which was odd because when I explained what I was doing, he looked incredulously and said, "So you're just a labourer, then!"

On my next visit, I very ostentatiously had with me the great ungainly tome of Beatrice and Sydney Webb, *Soviet Communism: A New Civilization?* If he wanted backsliding, I'd give it to him. I never managed to read the book, but it stirred things up a bit. "Going to be a communist now, then?" I beamed enigmatically.

Total despair set in when I announced that my next career move was to an Israeli Kibbutz to which I was to travel overland in a Land Rover owned by a fellow idealist with a legacy. There were three of us ex United Nations Association workers with Campaign for Nuclear Disarmament badges who set off from Bath on Pancake Day 1962 for Israel. This was a very important part of my education but I still had only one "O" Level on returning to Bath in 1962. I was interviewed about my Kibbutz experiences on BBC West for a fantastic eight guineas. One of my fellow travellers who was a member of the local Labour Party got taken on as Jim Callaghan's agent for the lead up to the 1964 election.

I decided to turn myself into a body acceptable for University in the UK. As I possessed only one "O" level which was Maths and I wished to study English Literature I had work to do! I spent two years to obtain University qualifications but failed to be accepted by a University. I wrote a letter to the newly opened Warwick University urging my case. Professor Hunter responded and offered me a place on his "English and American Literature" Course.

Being a very slow reader, I found the work hard and demanding but it was very rewarding to be in a world where ideas were explored and evaluated. Professor Hunter was a constant inspiration and encouragement. I particularly liked his forthrightness and his impatience with political correctness:

"Othello was as black as my boot!"

"What you have written, Mr. Bishop, is a tissue of nonsense."

It clearly was and I felt respected not insulted by his honesty. True, he did add: "Which is not like you," which was kind but I really did not need it. Surely, I cannot be the only one who respects and appreciates honest assessment. One would think so given the straitjacket of hyperbole which teachers are workshopped into in order not to offend the "customers." I sense that schoolchildren are desperate for realistic appraisal. They want to know where they are.

"Everyone Can Be a Genius at the Overseas Family School!"

This was the title of a ridiculous booklet handed out at that establishment in 1994. At that time we were in the thrall of a guru brought in as the very latest thing to promote "The Learning Revolution." Accelerated learning facilitated by a background of Baroque music was the mysticism under which kids were being abused at the time, and if, as a teacher, one did not enthusiastically embrace it, one was summarily dismissed. But I am getting ahead of myself.

I was eventually accepted as an English Teacher at a UK School.

Prior to this appointment, my CV reads: Insurance Clerk, National Service, Grocery Assistant, Assistant Youth Hostel Warden, United Nations Association general labourer, Bakery assistant, Plasticine Mixer, Betterwear Brush Salesman, Inserter of nuts into Wall's nut crunch (terminated abruptly when I launched nutless nut crunch by nodding off over the nut inserter), Newsagent's assistant, Kibbutznik, Wages' Clerk. I had to write to all of these employers to scrape together evidence that I had been gainfully employed, for a period of six years. As many of the jobs were very short term, a very odd bundle of documents were sent to Warwickshire County Council.

During this chequered career, the most difficult thing to bear had increasingly become the banality of casual conversation. The morning after the Soweto Massacre, I was working in the Chelsea Road, Bath branch of The co-operative Grocery Department. It felt like solitary confinement.

I was constantly aware of the "panic and emptiness" thinly concealed by the chatter which was background noise to daily life. I can clearly remember advancing to my position on the conveyor belt at Wall's Ice Cream Factory in Gloucester feeling positively suicidal. It must have shown for I had said nothing. A kindly lady, put her arm around my shoulders and said,

"Cheer up love, only another week and you're out of here."

And this from someone who was there for the long haul. What an amazing example of empathy.

So, I had made it out of the banality and could look forward to stimulating, intellectual staffroom exchanges.

It did not happen quite like that! So I will move on to my efforts to achieve what I thought of as being worthwhile.

After being at my first school for a few weeks a boy came into my classroom and said that the teacher named Claud wanted to see me in the next room.

I assumed that it was a matter of some urgency, set the class a task, and went into Claud's classroom. The boys in his class were sitting deathly quiet, heads bowed to the task before them. Claud directed me to a large desk in the front corner of the room in full view of the boys, and pointed. The desk was covered with the most explicit pornographic photographs imaginable. I was stunned. I really did not know what to do or say. The boys, were, obviously threatened by this person and I didn't know how to handle it. I'm not sure I do now. It was clear to me that there was a frisson for him setting out the display in the boys' presence. But he could easily wriggle out of that: he'd found the photographs and was wondering what to do about them. The people I did speak to about it just shrugged it off. Everyone knew he was a loud-mouthed obscenity.

Claud co-wrote and musically directed the annual school Revue which was hugely popular but, UNBELIEVABLE. He sat—I swear—begowned at a portable organ in front of the stage playing "The Stripper" whilst one of the boys in drag performed a striptease culminating in "her" throwing "her" wig to the audience. This in full view of the governors, the headmaster, and parents. If this was not deemed inappropriate, what could I do?

A distraught parent one parents' evening started to tell me how worried she was that Claud had groups of young boys to his home in the evenings, amongst them her son.

"He is, Mum, he's one of them!

I stopped her as professionalism dictated and told her that any concerns involving other members of staff should go straight to the Head. I do not know whether she expressed such concerns but subsequent events led me to believe she did and faced ranks closed against her.

The Headmaster used to enter to morning assembly from the back of the hall like the deus ex machina and everyone was expected to stand in awe. The staff all sat on the stage behind the Headmaster (after having stood in awe). After this particular assembly, the Headmaster announced the new dispensation, Mrs. X was to be the girls' counsellors, and . . .

". . . on Wednesdays, after school, Mr. Claud will make himself available to the boys."

The school erupted. The staff struggled bravely. Oh, Headmaster why were you the only one who didn't know? Perhaps it had something to do with keeping an open mind and coming to balanced decisions. Three years later, Claud who took the boys' judo club returned with his charges from a weekend judo camp. Some of the kids were in Chris X's form. He was asking a few of us how he should proceed. Chris had heard the boys discussing the fun they had had. Claud evidently was a real laugh. They had played hunt the keys (Claud's) which had to be hidden about one's person.

"Mr. Claud put them down the front of his underpants!"

We were at a loss and wandered impotently off to our lessons to mull over events. Later that day, Chris was called to the Headmaster's office. The staff room conversation had been overheard by the Head of Lower School, Stromboli had rumbled. As Chris X opened the Head's door, he saw Stromboli and the keys with the Head.

"Tell the Headmaster what you were saying in the staff room earlier Chris"

Claud was exonerated, Chris X reprimanded.

"As a bachelor, Claud is in a vulnerable position and we have to be very careful what we say."

Two years' later Claud was sentenced to two years for sexually assaulting boys. The sad tally of which I am aware at the High School was:

Claud—abuse of boys—two years in prison.

Head of French—married with two children—on overseas school trip accompanied by Miss X (single and of a certain age). Head of French leaves wife and two kids and shacks up with Miss X. Miss X promoted to Deputy Head.

Clive X—married with one child—caught at it with English teacher (ex-nun and proponent of teaching for life) whilst supervising holiday for underprivileged kids from Belfast.

Maths teacher picked up by police for propositioning boys in public lavatory—gaoled.

Dirk X sleeping and "smoking" with sixth-form girl—promoted.

Biology teacher—married, Catholic, seduces sixth form daughter of Classic's teacher—promoted.

People don't talk of the hidden curriculum any more, though it's still there.

I took charge of the Lower School Drama. My self-imposed task was to encourage the enthusiasm that exists amongst young kids for such activity. This necessitated writing most of the material myself. I wrote *Bug-Eyed Loonery* (since published by Samuel

French) which seeks to lampoon the situation as I saw it developing and to urge the important of imagination. I quote from it:

> Sycorax: But what of the future: the biggest threat [to Imagination] lies in the Land of Childhood. HE [an animated TV set] has captured that but can it be held? It is on the Land of Childhood that Imagination will make her strongest counter-attack. Therefore we must keep a vigilant watch on those who have influence there.
>
> 10th Loon: No problem there, O Sycorax. Not a spark of imagination to be found.
>
> 11th Loon: There is a story of which we can all be proud; Imagination will not be aided in the Land of Schoolteachers.
>
> 12th Loon: Unbelievable, O Sycorax is the foolishness of schoolteachers.
>
> 10th Loon: So vast are the schools that they have created that Imagination herself gets lost in their corridors.
>
> 11th Loon: So great is the bulk of paper used to pass messages to one another that the imaginations of hundreds of schoolteachers is crushed beneath its weight each week.
>
> 12th Loon: O Sycorax, the Land of Childhood is a pretty sight.
>
> 10th Loon: We are far advanced with our plan for the final solution of the Schoolteacher Problem.
>
> 11th Loon: One day soon, we shall herd them all into a colossal School.
>
> 12th Loon: Then we shall throw the key away.
>
> 10th Loon: And all the schoolteachers in the land will spend eternity passing messages to one another on little pieces of paper.[1]

Whenever I have seen it performed, there has always been sympathetic laughter. It was first performed in 1972 and apart from "little pieces of paper" being replaced by e-mails little has changed. The bureaucratization, for me, reached its apogee when I agreed to be teacher-in-charge of the three-week post–O Level programme. After exams, there were three weeks during which kids had to be gainfully occupied. I had to work out with 150 kids a

1. Bishop, *Bug-Eyed Loonery.*

personal project each which they were to work on on a daily basis, interspersed with visiting speakers and trips.

"Miss Freeman, Brian Bishop here. Please put me through to the Red Arrow 'Bus Company. I want to make sure that the coaches are booked out for Monday morning to take sixty-four students to London."

"Have you got permission to make a 'phone call from the Headmaster?"

"Well . . . No . . . but I'm trying to organize . . ."

"I can't put you through until you clear it with the Head."

"Are you refusing to put me through?"

"Well, I'll report this to the Head."

I put the 'phone down and charged to the Head's room. The Head would not put up with this!

"If I say a call is school business, I expect that to be good enough."

"Well . . . I wouldn't like to think you had that power."

"Who is, then, to decide?"

"Just give me a ring, and I'll decide."

Just what kind of professional did that make me!

Back to the staffroom from whence I rang the Headmaster.

"Hello, Headmaster, Brian Bishop here. I want to 'phone the Red Arrow Bus Company to ask whether the coaches to take us to the House of Commons are booked out for Monday morning. Can you tell me if this is school business?

"Yes, that is school business."

As I was putting the 'phone down, I heard ". . . er . . . Mr. Bishop . . ." I ignored it. This was the man who suggested that we should alter Blake's "Jerusalem" for assembly purposes because we should not encourage students to begin sentences with a conjunction. To my shame, I gave up the struggle. It is, as Paul found, hard to kick against the pricks. I would follow my writing career: I resigned.

Well, follow it I did, but my bank manager decided not to follow me, and the government of Singapore decided that I was needed to boost things up in their classrooms. The Singapore Ministry of Education decided to recruit English National Crème de la Crème teachers to show the locals how things should be done. Maybe this was not a bad idea but the practicalities were less easily grasped. What follows relates to how things were in 1986. I am told by Contacts still working there that what I write is still recognisable today.

If it's bureaucrats you want, go to Singapore. I loathe them! Singapore for me was a trial by fire. But I wouldn't have missed it for the world. As Keats tells us,

> To bear all naked truths,
> And to envisage circumstance, all calm,
> That is the top of sovereignty.[2]

Getting accepted was easy: one praised the multicultural harmony and order of the place in which it would be an honour to participate, and affected HUMILITY at such an economic miracle and so on. Getting in was a little more difficult. The sticking point in my case was that the bureaucrats did not have confirmation that I had actually worked at a Boys' School fifteen years earlier. Everything else was in order but until 1968–1970 were accounted for, we had deadlock. I 'phoned Warwickshire County Council. They asked me what I wanted them to say. I dictated it. They sent it off and we were on the plane.

There followed days of form filling, warnings, and exhortation at the Ministry of Education. We were told that unlike the UK where "you can be absent for no reason," in Lee Kuan Yew's Brave New World, you had to have a Certificate for every day's absence. The individual's account of their physical condition being equated with "no reason." In Singapore, the State and its agencies do the reasoning for you. All you have to do is as you are told. And woe betide you if you do not. As Lee said in the sixties when the Singapore Airlines pilots threatened to go on strike, "I'll teach them a lesson they'll never forget."[3] He mentioned treason and they changed their minds. Singapore executed more people per capita than anywhere else claiming democratic governance. Friday

2. Keats, "Hyperion," book 2.
3. See Okoth, "Lee Kuan Yew."

afternoon was execution time. We were shown films of the education system at work that were pure Leni Riefenstahl. It was quite disturbing. But then, a film of the National History Unit shown to the schoolchildren, which dealt with the Japanese occupation, showed the Japanese soldiers coming down the Malayan Peninsula on bicycles with the accompanying commentary:

> The British soldiers ran away so fast that the Japanese soldiers had to leap upon bicycles to catch up with them.

I could see that education was going to be a tall order. But I was not prepared for the cynical tearing up of our contracts. The Central Provident Fund which, we were told, mandated twenty per cent of our salaries per month as a contribution to be matched by twenty per cent from our employers—the Ministry of Education. This 40 per cent was to be held until we left Singapore and, therefore represented a very sizeable terminal bonus. 1986 saw the worst financial recession in Singapore's history. Lee decided (for he decided everything) that the CPF employers' contribution should be cut by nine percentage points. This was announced as our tyres hit the tarmac and there were to be no exceptions for "expats." In spite of their contracts. Now the official line was that the contracts allowed for this as there was a sentence which stated, "20 per cent or at rates to be determined from time to time by the government." We, of course, assumed that the rate at the beginning of the contract would hold good for the duration of that contract and this was indeed confirmed by a local lawyer who also told me, "You have a cut-and-dried case but forget it: there isn't a judge in Singapore who would find against the Government."

I didn't forget it. I campaigned long and hard for justice but that story is outside the scope of this book. I will just say that Mrs. R. Clousten, the person at the Ministry in charge of expat affairs told me, "What really hurts, Mr. Bishop, is that you say we must have known when you were interviewed in London. None of us knew or even guessed it as a remote possibility. Lee Kuan Yew, himself, at the last National Day Address said the CPF would never be touched: it was the sacred cow. This was the headline in "The Straits Times."

"So your Ministry's position is that we, in London, should have understood the possibility of the cut from the contract sentence you quote to us, when you, in Singapore, and employees of a Government Ministry did not regard it as a 'remote possibility'?"

She never replied. Later she was moved to another department and R. Lt. Colonel Peck took her place. The army were in position!

R, Mr. Wan Fook Wen, the Principal of The Anglo-Chinese Juniors College, greeted me when I arrived at my posting.

"Ah, Bishop. You will be in charge of rugby as your ECA."

"Fine. But you should know that I hate the game. Loathe its ethos. Don't know the rules."

"Ah . . . Very strange, Bishop. It's clearly registered on your CV."

God bless the bureaucrats. After holding up my application for so long for the vital information that I had taught in the town of Rugby in 1968, they had managed to transpose this to register me as an expert on the game of rugby! Wisdom prevailed and I was given Drama.

Cultural differences there were aplenty. The Ministry of Education, amazingly and for reasons I never discovered, did not check out our references. This was a grave error for the bunch of teachers shipped out from the UK was a very motley crew indeed. "The wretched refuse of your teeming shore," comes to mind.[4] We were a sorry bunch, refugees fleeing scandals of all kinds. One family: parents and two sons were right at the end of their tether. The father appeared quite proud of the fact that they had had breakfast on the morning of departure, left the washing-up and no forwarding address, for the house to be repossessed by the mortgage company. The sexual and alcohol excesses which had got out of hand in the UK were to be given a fresh start in Singapore. At the "Col Bar" on Friday night there was to be seen drunkenness of Hogarthian proportions. There were people picked up and

4. Lazarus, "New Colossus."

deported for having no qualifications when suspicions eventually gave rise to checks; people disappearing overnight without paying their taxes; wives being left for teenage students, of both sexes, who had been impregnated and an assortment of inadequates looking for haven. It was, at that time, not a career move except perhaps for people like Billy who came to me one night after closing time to check on parts of speech? He was being inspected and had no idea what the parts of speech were. He was now Head of English at the Chinese High School and adviser to the Ministry of Education on the teaching of English Language. So what was in it for Singapore? Well, Lee Kuan Yew, who else, was appalled by the standard of spoken English amongst the local population. It is indeed appalling but has since been dignified by various Language "experts" on visiting meal tickets as "Singlish," so now all is well. However, Mr. Lee decided something must be done: the Ministry must recruit Super Teachers from the country where the Queen's English was spoken. And here we were! Good Ideas are one thing, implementing them quite another.

People tried and some worked hard and conscientiously, but it was difficult not to have the stuffing knocked out of you by the dead hand of bureaucratic control. There was the "Buku Guru," and still is, into which details of each lesson had to be written at the beginning of the week and deviations had to be explained if reported. Some Principals were of sufficient seniority and wisdom to apply the rules with discretion. Such was Wan Fook Wen. He used to talk in the third person and deliver utterances like a modern day Confucius:

"Mr. Wan says, 'If life can be simple, why make it difficult?'"

Thus we did not have lessons on Saturday mornings as younger Principals trying to impress with the diligence of their establishments did. He claimed to understand expats and indulged their idiosyncrasies. He once barked at a local teacher, thrusting a white envelope in his face, "I am the Principal. If I say this envelope is red, it is red!"

He would never do that to an expat teacher, but it is indicative that he thought this an appropriate way to talk to locals. Authority was everything and it had to be conferred and was never assumed; thus acting on one's own initiative was an alien concept. An acquaintance working as a civil engineer on the Mass Rapid Transport System (MRT), Singapore's very impressive underground system which was developed whilst we were there, asked one of his local colleagues to remove a lamppost which was blocking progress. He recoiled at the idea as it was not on the specification. Andy jumped into the digger, drove it into the post and said, "Oops!" whilst the local engineers looked on with awe. This was typical. But Mr. Wan admired that kind of initiative. Howard, the rugby man, told me that he heard Wan at the dining table defend me against locals' complaints that I was rather aggressive in the way I approached things.

"Bishop gets things done, lah!"

Thanks for that, Fook Wen. I wouldn't have lasted five minutes under some of the regimes tolerated by some of my colleagues. Wan Fook Wen was special. I wonder if there is a connection between him and my colleagues who were superseded by a new generation in the sixties. He was of similar age and had experienced the Japanese occupation. He recalled queuing for hours in the hot sun to receive a crust of stale bread. He told me that he used to ingratiate himself with the Japanese soldiers as a boy by climbing up mango trees and throwing them the fruit. When you've had experiences like that, you see bullshit a mile off. I liked him a lot. He wrote me the most glowing testimonial I have ever received, supporting my request to the Ministry of Education for reinstatement of my CPF (in vain). Well. I say he wrote it. I asked him to do so and he said, "Your English better than mine, Bishop. You write it, I'll sign, lah!"

I decided to go on the offensive. The stage at ACJC was a marvellous theatre space and the auditorium seated two thousand every Monday for a religious (Methodist) service.

There was an assembly every morning outside on the parade ground where we sang the National Anthem and saluted the flag. However, the stage lighting and the curtains in the hall were a mess. The stage had twelve fly lines, more than the Victoria Theatre that, at the time, was the main Theatre in Singapore. But, there was no fly tower, so the lines went nowhere. There was a front lighting bar way up in the auditorium roof at about forty feet where it was impossible to get at to change or set the lights. The sound system was chaotic. This was symbolic of the prevalent local approach: go for the prestigious rather than the functional: just look at the number of Mercedes and BMW's on tiny Singapore with huge car tax disincentives. It's called Kiasu which is a Hokkien adjective literally meaning afraid of losing. It is possibly Singapore's defining characteristic. I priced the refurbishment of the facility: remotely-controlled lighting, sound and curtains with a hydraulically operated front lighting bar. Wan Fook Wen thought it was a good idea and agreed that if I could raise half the money, the Government would, by an existing arrangement, provide the other half. I got a group of expats together with some local staff and revived *Sweeney Todd*. I mounted an energetic publicity campaign; I manned a ticket booth every lunchtime. I sold about twenty tickets. This looked to be a no-hoper. Then the discipline master (every school had them) returned from leave of absence and took over the ticket sales. Every class representative was called to a meeting. The tickets were divided between them, and they were told the tickets would be sold and the money collected in a fortnight's time. Every ticket was sold, all three thousand of them: five performances to a 600 audience. I had had another lesson in the Singapore authoritarian approach. Nobody seemed resentful: they just did as they were told, but the downside was, until told, they did nothing.

No one was trusted either and therefore, until threatened, didn't perceive a line to toe. There is no graffiti in Singapore: they cane you if you attempt it. There are no guns in Singapore: they hang you if you're caught with one, whether you are using it or not. Taxi drivers used to laugh incredulously when we, sitting in the back seats, used to put on seat belts.

"No need, lah. Only compulsory in front seats. Ha! Ha! Only expats use."

It is now compulsory. Taxi drivers are fined if passengers are not using them. They now have notices all over their cabs threatening passengers. All the tickets for *Sweeney Todd* had to be taken to the Ministry of Community Development and every one of them had to be stamped and registered to ensure there was no corruption. It took forever. My frustration showed.

"Ah, you never done this before, lah"

"I've spent my life doing it, but I've never done it in Singapore before."

It was not long before I realised that this was one and the same thing. This system has now been changed.

R. Onora O'Neill, in the 2002 Reith Lectures, reminded us that Confucius told his disciple Tsze-kung that three things are needed for government: weapons, food and trust. Trust should be discarded last: "without trust we cannot stand."[5] It is strange that Singapore, largely Chinese, has not taken the master's wisdom on board. However, being made acutely aware of this lack of trust as a way of life, crystallised for me what was becoming the soul-destroying norm in education: the attempt to make teachers accountable for every move they make exacerbates what Doctor O'Neill called our "crisis of trust."[6]

The tunnellers working on the Mass Rapid Transport System (MRT) were also expats as the skill was not available locally: therefore they could not be beaten into submission. They began working to rule by stopping dead at 5:00 pm. without pumping out the tunnels. They also had a very astute and highly placed local representative. Shortly after the "*NO EXCEPTIONS FOR EXPATS!*" *Straits Times* headline, there appeared another: "*MRT MEN AN EXCEPTION SAYS MINISTRY OF FINANCE.*" We had no tunnels to flood. In any case, people were lining up to escape from British classroom lunacy and the Ministry of Education Bureaucrats were limited on the discrimination front as indicated by my rugby experience and Friday nights at "The Col Bar."

The day-to-day teaching was less than exhilarating. The students sat there writing down one's every word. Classroom contributions were an alien concept. I had the top academic class of 17 to 18 year-olds for General Paper. GP was rather like General

5. O'Neill, *Question of Trust*, 3.

6. O'Neill, *Question of Trust*, 4.

Studies but it was required to pass this paper to be accepted by The National University of Singapore. Clearly, the class had to be encouraged to debate and offer and defend opinions. I managed to get some ideas from the students regarding the recent election of Corizan Aquino in the Philippines after the EDSA revolution; was it a positive vote for her or a negative vote against Marcos? The ideas dried up and there being a few minutes remaining, I switched attention to the local financial crisis: was it being dealt with sensibly. There were a few ideas exchanged, someone said that they thought the Government were placing too much of the burden on the workers with their CPF cuts whereas management was to some degree responsible for the situation. The bell went and we departed. As I reached the lift to descend to the ground floor, a group of agitated 18 year-old boys caught up with me.

"You won't tell on us, sir, will you?"

"Sorry, what do you mean?"

"Well. We're not supposed to talk about politics."

These were the brightest lads in the college, among them R. Stanley Peck, the winner of the Singapore schools' Maths prize two years in succession and national representative in London at the International Students' Maths Conference. They were genuinely frightened.

Lee Kuan Yew, his wife, and son went to Cambridge. Therefore Singapore has a special relationship with Cambridge. "O" Level is continued in Singapore. The rest of the world does IGCSE (International General Certificate of Secondary Education). All local schools do Cambridge "A" Levels. No other schools in Singapore are allowed to do Cambridge "A" Levels. Why is this? It, like many things in Singapore, is a mystery outside the enchanted circle. We can draw our own conclusions, but, according to the inscrutable Mr. Wan, we must not give them utterance. There is an annual school farce in Singapore. All students sit the November Cambridge "O" and "A" Level examinations. The school year starts on the first of January. The "O" Level results are published by Cambridge in January. They go not to the students, not to the schools, but to the Ministry of Education. And there they stay until March/

April. Meanwhile, of course, secondary school students have to be assigned Junior College Places at which to study for the Cambridge "A" Levels. There is much competition as there is a very generally perceived hierarchy of colleges with Raffles' Junior College at the top. They are assigned on their predicted grades. These bear no, or very little, relationship to their actual results; so in April it is all change and the first three months teaching has to be general with nobody taking it seriously as the actual "A" Level courses the students are allowed to take are determined by the college to which they are eventually assigned. I, in fact, spent the first three months without any teaching whatsoever assigned to me.

"Predicted results bear no relationship to actual results, lah!"
"It would seem then, Mr. Wan, that either the results are faulty or the system of predicting needs some attention."

After much hilarity. "Ha! Ha! Bishop. In Singapore it is dangerous to draw conclusions. Mr. Wan prefers to say, 'No relation, lah!'"

So no relation, lah, it was.

But what are those results, both "A" and "O" Level doing at the Ministry all that time, maturing? I draw no conclusions, Mr. Wan. I simply tell you that of the students I taught, 96 per cent passed "A" Level and, in my judgement, most of them were not of "O" Level standard. I refused to spoon feed them as many did and my lessons were based on the clearly understood assumption that the students had read the books. I well remember a day or two before the examination one year, a very giggly and embarrassed girl arrived at the staff room door and asked me for a study aid of a certain book that she admitted never having read. I said that I did not use them and did not know of one but that she should have read the book. She claimed to be speaking for most of the class of some 30 students when she said that none of them had read the book. To which I replied, "Then you will all fail." They all passed. One of the local English Teachers had a copy of *All Creatures Great and Small* on her desk. She was constantly reading it. She was very limited in her response to literature. She was a Cambridge Graduate and claimed that her interview had been conducted around Herriot's book.

I continued to work my socks off directing *The Diary of Anne Frank* in my second year.

This was made rather special by the fact that Anne was played by a Malay girl, her father by a Chinese boy, and her mother by an Indian girl. It gave an added poignancy and universality to the terrible events recorded by that play. This was acknowledged by the First Secretary at the Embassy of Israel who wrote a letter of congratulations after seeing the play. The sound effects called for by the script are crucial in establishing the world of normality which is the background to these terrible events: we are not in a capsule of evil; we are in the world inhabited by you and I. These effects were recorded by the excellent Bristol Old Vic which had one of the best rep companies in England and is now reduced to a touring house. The play was chosen to open the Singapore Arts Festival that year at the Singapore Labour Foundation Auditorium. I was approached by local teachers with advice on how to improve the production for this occasion. I didn't use the flashback technique of the original script preferring to use the one set of the warehouse attic. Thus, my ending consisted of the cast quietly gathering their few belongings as the effect of the Nazi soldiers shouting, ringing the buzzer, hammering on and eventually breaking-down the doors is played. The characters all lined up front stage with Mr. Frank and then one by one left the stage as Mr. Frank makes the final speech concerning the fate of each one of them. It is intensely moving.

"We hope that you will change ending: very good play but ending bit anti-climax, lah!"

"Oh, what do you suggest?"

"Nazis should break down door and rush on in uniforms, drag off everybody, screaming."

Another devotee of the drama thought it would be spiced up if set to music: "Make a good musical, lah!"

Te Doh! I said nothing.

I had some help building the set but, apart from that, nothing. Shortly after, I was asked if I would assist the junior school with one of their productions. When I looked at their proposal, I discovered that they had assigned production jobs to 80 members of their staff. This was the way the local system seemed to operate: everyone must be involved and involvement meant giving most people non-jobs that simply meant their time was not their own. I was, despite Mr. Wan's philosophy, told to report to Mac Ritchie Reservoir at 8:00 am one Saturday morning where all staff were to help with the school's canoe carnival. I turned up bleary-eyed to discover that my job was to read out the names of half of the winners whilst someone else's job was to read out the other half. These were jobs of about two minutes each at the end of the morning. I told the organiser that if there was a proper job for me to do I would be happy to do it, but if they were going to insult me in this way, I was not staying. I left with shouts of, "I'll report you to the Principal," hurled at my back. I guess this is what was meant by my aggressive approach whereas the aggression seemed to me to be coming at me not from me. I was, in short, experiencing the undermining of my professional pride and integrity that Dr. O'Neill, in the Reith Lectures to which I have referred, said would follow from a "culture of suspicion,"[7] although she had not yet said it! I had arrived at the professional cynicism to which she feared it might lead. All my National Service training came into play: I became a skiver, leaning on the monsoon drain rail, smoking Marlborough cigarettes with R. Howard Clements and generally taking the piss out of everyone and everything. It all seemed so pointless. When, one morning, Howard got excited by the fact that a gnarled old tree trunk on the other side of the monsoon drain had a striking sensuality resembling the nether regions of the female body, I realised something had to be done. I was playing Doctor Faustus in Marlowe's play at the Singapore stage club at the time and as I appeared to have spent so many of my free hours walking the amateur boards, why not try to translate this activity into a living? I would become an actor.

At the age of fifty, this idea was not on all occasions treated with respect, particularly by my Mother-in-Law. However, I pressed on and was offered a place at The Mountview Theatre

7. O'Neill, *Question of Trust*, 17.

School', Wood Green, London, on their post-graduate acting course. Our house was put on the market to finance the enterprise and, in the meantime, I took out a GBP 5,000 Career Development Loan from Barclay's Bank to pay the fees (GBP 6,000 payable in two instalments). A few weeks into the first term, the house decided to do something it had resisted for sixty-odd years—subside. This proved not to be a great selling point. Mountview were pressing for the second instalment of fees. I said that I had only done a bit of one term. I had been told that the GBP 3,000 I had paid was for two terms.

They said that this was true but they had omitted to point out that the two terms for which I had paid were the first and the last terms, so second term's fees were now required. R. Judi Dench, patron of the School (now an Academy, I note) intervened on my behalf in vain. I had a letter from her hoping that I find a suitable outlet for my talent; the jury is still out on that one. I would have to leave "Mountview" and try to get work without graduating from an accredited school. This meant that I would have to be doubly attractive as a director would have to release one of his few available Equity cards to employ me; as a graduate, this was waived. So the mug-shot went into "Spotlight" and I was up for grabs. I experienced some odd moments and some amazing promises (unfulfilled).

I took myself along at some considerable expense to R. Michael McCallion of *The Voice Book* and acting tutor at RADA for many years. He observed my pieces and was extremely positive about them.

One was a piece from *The Entertainer* to which he responded, "That was a better interpretation than Olivier's and gave reasons for so saying. Being of a sceptical not to say cynical cast of mind by this time, I assumed his judgement to be, perhaps subconsciously, influenced by the prospect of further lucrative lessons. He, in fact, wrote me a reference, and said he would be pleased to give me further lessons free of charge, not as charity but until I got work, "As you assuredly will, when you can pay me back." That seemed to be it. Jenny and I went to the evening performance at the Old Vic in good spirits. Two weeks later I 'phoned to discover that Michael's eyeballs had ruptured and that he was in a Swiss clinic indefinitely.

From out of the sky I distinctly heard a voice cry, "BACK TO TEACHING, MY SON!" It was my Bank Manager's.

I managed to get a long-term sickness cover at Redland High School, Bristol in September 1990. The lady concerned had been advised not to return as she had a serious heart condition. She chose to ignore medical advice and I was out of work again. I had picked up the information that there was something of a drama crisis as the Head of English had decided that the traditional Christmas production was beyond his powers. I approached the Headmistress, R. Carol Lear, and passed on my opinion that such a school should be mounting a production at least once a year. Her enthusiastic assent encouraged me to suggest that she might think of employing an outside director as the school could not produce one and that I was her man. I expected a rebuff if not derisive laughter, but Carol asked me to come back tomorrow with a plan and a price. I returned saying that I would produce and direct *A Midsummer Night's Dream* at the end of the Christmas Term and my fee would be GBP 1,000. Carol said that she thought I might say that, although she was hoping for GBP 500. I pointed out that Peter Hall would charge more and she restored my faith in educational administrators by cheerfully agreeing saying that she thought the value of such activities was incalculable and she would deal with the Governors. I thought back to 1984 at Red Maids an open-air production of *A Midsummer Night's Dream* with a professional orchestra accompaniment playing Mendelssohn's score and the Governor's "support."

Clearly, there was no future in peripatetically directing *A Midsummer Night's Dream* so, following the example of other notable fascists, I escaped to South America—Peru, to be precise, Colegio San Silvestre, Mira Flores, Lima had a problem. They had recently appointed a Head of English who was inconsiderate enough to have a heart attack on arrival. For the start of their year in February 1991, they required another Head of English plus an English teacher. Jenny and I were interviewed by R. Peter Gummer at Gabbitas, Truman, and Thring in Piccadilly and hired on three-year contracts. Two years later in April 1993, I was sacked for disciplinary reasons so serious as to forfeit all contractual bonus rights and the statutory three-month's notice. I have decided to start this episode with the denouement, like a Greek tragedy, to see if I can make some sense of it that way around.

Colegio San Silvestre was founded in 1938, the year of my birth and, like me, it was a little creaky. I inherited a department in which two of the members were the Headmistress, R. Rina Bayly, and the Deputy Head, R. Dick Holt. Both of these had previously been Heads of the English Department, Dick, immediately prior to the appointment of the man who had suffered the heart attack. Dick had a B. Ed in Drama and Social Studies and had been teaching in the Elementary School as a classroom teacher when a crisis in the Senior School led to him being co-opted there as a senior school English teacher. He was later promoted to Head of English, and, according to Rina, was very reluctant to surrender the role. The long-serving-teacher pool in such places is not very large and crises are frequent. Those who, like Dick, stick it out uncritically and, in his words, "take the rough with the smooth" are invaluable and loyalty points accrue. Rina had also taken over in a crisis. She was Head of English when the previous Head of School, who was a dipsomaniac and subject of many affectionate anecdotes, disappeared overnight. The common assumption was that her husband was under threat from Sendero Luminoso—the Maoist Shining Path Guerillas who were in their dubious pomp at the time.

Dick, who had assigned himself the top set preparing for Cambridge IGCSE Language and Literature, had difficulties to which he occasionally admitted. There was one particular instance when a girl came to me in the staff room, having been dispatched from Dick's double lesson to ask if I could come and talk to the class on F. T. Prince's poem "Soldiers Bathing." I said that I would be along in fifteen minutes after looking at the poem and arrived with one-hour of the lesson left during which I went through the poem looking at the language and imagery and attempting to identify the central challenging idea of that remarkable poem. Dick came to me afterwards to thank me in a very genuine, heartfelt fashion. He confessed, "We have been looking at it for weeks and have got nowhere." I respected his honesty, but my performance, although appreciated, cannot have made Dick feel more at ease with himself or with me. The school was in the process of transferring allegiance to The International Baccalaureate and part of my task was to initiate the English course leading up to Language A2 (that Language A1 was not to be attempted will tell you about the reality of the "bilingual" nature of the school). I looked at the syllabus and devised a course which had to be submitted to Dick who was to be the IB Coordinator. He wrote back saying that he had been through my suggestions "backward, forward, upside down looking for faults and omissions but could find none." Dick admitted at his coordinator meetings to being very anxious—"I am in awe of this examination." This anxiety communicated itself to the guinea pigs who confessed to me that they were very worried as "none of the teachers seem to know what they are doing." All I could do was assure them that I knew exactly what I was doing and that, as far as English went, they could relax. Again, as all such utterances find their way back to other members of staff, this did not help to make me Mr. Popular.

Rina was married to R. Tim who was a manager of Crystal Brewery

I thought that I had a good relationship with Rina as she used to engage me in friendly banter often involving robust comments on the inadequacies of male members of staff and seeking my support in propping-up the system. For example, she required someone to take on the role as examination co-ordinator telling me M was the obvious candidate as he had no other responsibility, "But he is completely incompetent." He has since been awarded an OBE for services to education. I was Head of English, responsible for the Magazine, and school Drama. I now became examinations co-ordinator. I felt acutely embarrassed by the fact that we—ex-pats—were thought to be worthy of very much better pay and conditions than local staff. The opportunity to demonstrate some kind of solidarity presented itself in very sad circumstances. One of the local members of staff had a three-year-old daughter, R. Claudia, who was diagnosed with a brain tumour and the prognosis was very poor. The parents, of course, were exhausting all possible avenues, involving trips to specialists in North America and so on. All this was very expensive and they had no medical insurance. I decided to resurrect *Sweeney Todd* as an expat staff production, the proceeds to go towards Claudia's medical expenses. Rina agreed to play Mrs. Lovett to my Sweeney and Dick, Jonas Fogg, the keeper of the madhouse. Jenny, ever a flattering critic of my performances, is convinced that my role was played so convincingly that Rina developed a morbid fear of me (this indicates the level of our incredulity at subsequent events). We raised $2,000 and I was amazed to be called in to Rina's office. Dick had already told me that he did not hold with all this "giving to charity." There had obviously been some discussion as Rina asked me if I wanted all of the money to go to Claudia, or should half of it go to the school. I pointed out that I had co-opted people on the understanding that it was to be Claudia's money and Rina withdrew. Little Claudia went through a period of, what turned out to be, recession, and Jenny and I were invited to a picnic by a lake with her and her parents. As we watched her running around, she began to stagger and it was clear that the illness was reasserting itself. Watching her excitement at being taken out in a rowing boat by her father to feed the ducks was very poignant, the circumstances turning what is a very common delightful moment into a moment of unbearable sadness. Claudia died shortly afterwards.

I noticed that many of the senior students were printing in a way that gave their written work a very immature appearance and wondered if we ought to launch a campaign to encourage them to do joined-up writing. As we were talking about 16 and 17 year-olds, I thought that this was not going to be a controversial issue. I raised it at an English Departmental meeting and was immediately the victim of an attack launched with great energy by Dick and Rina. I was accused of imposing irrelevant values on the creative writing process and generally attempting to straitjacket young minds into my own outdated sense of decorum. I didn't know what to say: I was in the position of having to defend a position that I thought was long established and found myself talking about writing speed (pooh poohed), first impressions (ridiculed as shallow), and having my true fascist intentions exposed for all to see. Everyone else went off to their lessons and I was left cornered in the staff-room with Rina. She scrawled something illegible on a piece of paper and said, "OK, what would be your fist impressions of someone who signed a letter like that?"

I muttered something about it indicating someone who was not interested in presentation and careless of what others thought of him etc. etc.

"You know absolutely nothing about my husband. Who do you think you are passing judgement on someone you know nothing about?"

And she went on to tell me tearfully what a truly remarkable man she had married and I was made to feel unworthy to untie his shoelaces. I went to my lesson reeling. How had a simple suggestion that sending the girls out into world writing in a mature way might be helpful ended in me insulting Rina's husband? What on earth was going on I have no idea, but I was in the middle of it and it was rather threatening. I felt like a character in a Kafka novel.

About a year passed by and I was approaching the final rehearsals of another revival: *The Diary of Anne Frank*. I had a rehearsal at 5:00 pm. Rina called a "very important Heads of Departments Meeting" from which I could not be excused. We all assembled around the Conference Room Table and waited to be told what this urgent matter was.

"I have been thinking that something needs to be done about the girls' handwriting. Some of them are still printing and I would like your thoughts about launching a Campaign to get everyone to do joined-up writing."

I could not believe what I was hearing. I was tense regarding the production I was working on and I freely admit that my response was not positive. I kept absolutely quiet, not trusting my control of what might come out of my mouth. I was not allowed the security of my discretion.

"What do you think, Brian?"

"I do not believe what I am hearing, Rina. We've done all this and it ended up by you accusing me of insulting your husband. You know exactly what I think and I've nothing more to add. Can I please get on with my rehearsal?"

Clearly, this was a mistake as Rina had only to brazen it out to have everyone else, not having the faintest idea what I was talking about, perceive me as a raving lunatic. Dick, of course, knew, but Dick also knew upon which side Dick's bread was buttered. Word of my outburst was carried back to the staff, and Rina put it about sympathetically that she suspected me of schizophrenia. This was based upon the fact that she had come into the rehearsal room shortly after the meeting had closed to find me calmly directing rather than laying about the girls with a hatchet as my behaviour at the meeting, evidently, led her to fear (perhaps Jenny's *Sweeney Todd* theory has some mileage in it after all!). If Rina could present me to her mind as an inadequate, it would seem, she could accept me. Which brings me to Ivor Leighton. He was an elementary school teacher, escaping a failed marriage in England and the fact that he had impregnated his best friend's wife. He took-up with and married a kindergarten teacher who had come out in the same group. We were all friends and tended to gather at "The Brenchley Arms" a British pub, open all hours and run by Mike, a veteran of two Northern Ireland tours with the British Army. I was preparing for bed one night when I received a 'phone call from "The Brenchley Arms." It was a very agitated Ivor who wanted to talk with me. I said that I was off to bed and asked was it urgent enough for me to change my plans. He said that it was. So I dressed and set off down Avenida Jose Pardoe. What a tale he had to tell and how incompetently he had dealt with it! His wife Sandra, was with him. Evidently a group of girls in his class of sevenyear-olds were disrupting the lesson by passing around a note over which they were giggling. Ivor confiscated the note which was written in Spanish and therefore incomprehensible to him. The girls refused to translate, so he said that he would give the letter to the elementary Headmistress to translate for him. This triggered the following response:

> Girl One: I would not do that if I were you.
>
> Ivor: Oh, and why is that?
>
> Girl One: If you do, we will tell Miss [. . .] and our parents that you have been touching me where you shouldn't.
>
> Girl Two: Yes, and I saw you do it.
>
> Girl Three: And so did I.

I'll just remind you that we are in a class of seven-year-olds in a rather exclusive British girls' school in Lima, Peru, not in a 1920s New York Speakeasy. Would you not have thought that Ivor would have taken the girls and the note straight to the Headmistress and told her the story? Ivor was thinking of getting the next plane out of the country, convinced that Rina would believe the girls, he would be ignominiously dismissed and would never work again as a teacher. I took Ivor and Sandra back to our apartment and, having established that there was no truth in the accusation and that Ivor had never been alone with the three girls, it took Jenny and I until two in the morning to persuade him that the only way forward was to go to Rina with the story otherwise he was likely to bring about what he sought to avoid. I promised him that she would support him, that the girls would most likely be expelled, but that he certainly would not be asked to teach them again. In the UK under such circumstances it is accepted practice for one's union representative to attend as an objective third party for obvious reasons. This would be welcomed by both parties, again, for very obvious reasons.

I told Ivor that if he so wished, I would attend the meeting in the absence of a union representative. The meeting was set with Ivor facing his Headmistress and Rina. Rina was very agitated by my presence and after a short while asked me to leave saying she was quite capable of dealing with the situation without my assistance. I asked Ivor if he wanted me to leave and he, seeing which way the wind was blowing, said he did. I withdrew. After school that day I was called to Rina's office where she was livid with anger. She had never, in her whole career, had her integrity impugned in this manner and on and on. I asked if I might be permitted a word and pointed out that short of impugning her integrity, it was I who had convinced Ivor of that integrity and talked him out of running away. I said that the objective observer was common practice in such cases and presented a scenario where the girls' parents became involved convinced of their daughters' veracity and demanding Ivor's instant dismissal. Rina became very self-righteous and said that in such circumstances, "I would support Ivor to the hilt even if it meant putting my job on the line!"

I told her that I accepted this to be the case and my urging it had been instrumental in persuading Ivor to stay. But surely she might see that Ivor felt somewhat insecure. Rina's anger subsided somewhat. However, the girls were simply admonished for their naughtiness and Ivor had the indignity of having to continue with them facing him every morning with smirks on their faces. Ivor was not in Rina's "A" team.

Jenny and I took a holiday out of Lima. We flew over the Andes, back to Lima. We had been in a few minutes. Knock on door. "Are you Brian Bishop?"

"Yes."

"I have to give you this."

I was handed a legal document informing me that I had been dismissed for disciplinary reasons having "Spoken to the Headmistress in a chiding manner."

My employment pass was to be rescinded. There was to be no bonus payment nor payment in lieu of notice owing to the seriousness of the crime. I was to be out of the country within two weeks. I was to report to a meeting at the School tomorrow (Saturday) morning. Effectively, of course Jenny had been sacked too.

The following day, I duly reported to find a very serious Rina and R. Colin Derbyshire awaiting me. Colin spoke. Rina looked as if she were about to be sick.

"You know what has happened. You have been dismissed. I just wanted to say it to your face."

"Well, thank you for that, Colin. You have obviously heard Rina's version of events. I have written here my version. Perhaps I could read it to you."

Colin became animated waving his hands about for emphasis: "I don't want to hear it! I don't want to hear it! I don't want to hear it!"

I gathered he didn't want to hear it and asked him why, that being the case, he had asked me to a meeting. I pointed out that there were procedures for this sort of thing and I thought I ought to be allowed a hearing as sanctioned by the culture from which we all came. Rina spoke to her shame.

"We're not in England now, Brian. This is Peru, and I can do what I like."

I was approached by the Director of Studies at Newton College, Peru, who said that they were looking for a Head of English and, from what he knew of me, I would fit the bill.

"Before we go any further will you please answer one question: Did you at any time call Rina a lying bitch?"

He knew I hadn't as he knew all the other teachers involved. But if he had to ask such a question it was a road down which it was pointless for me travel. I withdrew.

The British Council put me in touch with R. Sr. Mountanto. Evidently, he was the top man in local labour disputes. He was happy to take the case on a no win no pay basis. It would take at least two years and I had to be in Peru for proceedings to take place. R. Bill Baker who was the head of Markham College our associated Boys School advised that if I went to court, I would lose.

"It has nothing to do with the merits of the case, Brian. It is about influence: they have it and you don't. It is not right, but that is the way things are here. You will lose."

Jenny and I relented. Rina had told the staff that she had a letter from the UK saying that I was not fit to be a teacher.

I remained intrigued as to what this letter was that Rina had claimed reported me as unfit to be a teacher. I met the person, a member of the English Department and former colleague, who had agreed to take over my role as Head of Department and he told me that she had shown him the letter to encourage him to subdue his qualms about taking advantage of my demise. It, he claimed, said that I was not really a teacher but a frustrated actor who carried my sense of resentment around with me. The writer had no evidence of me not getting on with females (why had she been asked this question?) as I had had no clashes in the writer's experience, "but perhaps that is because no females crossed him." I asked my replacement if he had seen whom it was from. He had not, but it was, he told me, headed

> CHELTENHAM LADIES' COLLEGE
>
> "Et tu, ENID!"
>
> R. Enid Castle was the headmistress at this school. I had served under her headship at another school. I wrote to Enid telling her the use to which her handiwork had been put and suggesting that the comment about me being not guilty of skirmishes with females on her watch perhaps because they had not crossed me was tantamount to a hiding to nothing. She wrote back shocked that her *"innocuous"* comments had been interpreted as support for sacking me and hoping etc. etc. I would love to have seen the letter she wrote to Rina regarding her appalling lack of professionalism. Perhaps Enid did not know the San Silvestre motto:
>
> "I AM, I CAN, I OUGHT, I WILL."

Three out of four ain't bad, Rina.

We arrived back in England to lick our wounds and look about us. I contacted R. Peter Gummer at "Gabbitas Truman and Thring" for confirmation of my opinion that I was now in outer darkness as far as they were concerned. *Not at all*, came the response. Evidently, personality clashes (so that's what it was!) were common and usually resolved by a switch to another school. It so happened that he had just the job for us at St. George's in Argentina: *Head of English and English teacher.* There was no need to come up to London for interview as he had already interviewed us. We were on our way!

Oh, yes we were!

Oh, no we weren't!

She's behind you!

Rina had put the block on me working on the same continent! She had agreed not to refer to my sacking if approached for a reference . . . unless, it seems, the job was in South America.

"You had better forget, South America, mate," said Peter Gummer.

Never mind Sweeney Todd, I felt like Count Dracula!

The previous February (1993), we had dropped in to the *European Council for International Schools' (ECIS)* Fair in Marble Arch to see what was on offer. Here we met R. Jenny Gaye who had been our younger daughter's "A" Level English teacher at the *International School of Singapore (ISS)* some three years previously. She was now employed by a new school that had been set up in Singapore in 1991 called *The Overseas Family School (OFS)!* She was the Headmistress and was looking for someone to teach "A" Level English and to be Head of Department. Evidently, it was a proprietor-led school, the Proprietor being a New Zealand man. R. David Perry. I understood that he was an accountant who had been brought in to sort out the mess at ISS after the Head had absconded with the funds. Having done this, he had decided to set up his own international school taking with him Jenny, as Principal and, R. Irene Chee, whom Sharon remembered as the photocopying lady at the *International School.* Irene was the CEO of the new school. According to Jenny, this was causing some teething problems as, although having no background in education, David and Irene were determined to exercise rigid top-down management of their new baby and had, evidently, decided that the problems at the *International School* had arisen from loss of that control. Thus any delegation was seen as dissipation of control. Heads of Department, therefore, presented themselves to their minds as little power bases and, as such, a threat to their authority. David had evidently declared that there would be Heads of Department "*over my dead body.*" Jenny, at the time, was dismissing this as a temporary aberration as, "Of course, you can't run a school without Heads of Department."

It was just a question of time before this was realized. Interesting stuff but we were not actively looking for a move, our contracts at San Silvestre having another year to run. So we wished Jenny well and went on our way. Now, of course, things were different and I contacted Jenny to see if the job was still open. It was and her deputy, R. Richard Allen, from Port Talbot, was currently at *Bath University* attending an MA summer school. I was to go there to talk with him. He conducted an interview and I was offered the job of "A" Level English Teacher with prospects. We returned to Singapore in August 1993. The minute nature of the control to be exercised over my life for the next 11 years became immediately apparent when we set about finding accommodation. My contract spoke of a S$2,000 per month housing allowance but, it transpired, I was not to receive this. I was to find accommodation and, if approved by Irene Chee, the school would pay the rent directly to the landlord.

Well . . . at least we thought, I was to be paid full CPF by OFS (20 per cent) as mandated by a Government now out of recession. And there it was in my pay for August and September 1993, the beginnings of a retirement package. Then I met this taxi driver who took great delight in disabusing me: "When you 55, employers CPF cut to 7.5 per cent, lah."

I was 55 in November. They couldn't, they wouldn't! Then the motto of San Silvestre rang loudly in my ears: "I AM, I CAN, I OUGHT, I WILL."

Evidently, the retiring age in Singapore was 55. The government introduced legislation to allow employers to pay only 7.5 per cent CPF to people over 55 to encourage them to keep such people in employment. Unusually for Singapore, it was not compulsory, in fact they requested that businesses doing well should not take advantage of the legislation to cut wages. I went to see Richard who had interviewed me in Bath and confirmed that I had understood things correctly: I had been promised 20 per cent CPF with no reference to 55 by him or the Handbook giving contractual details.

"Oh no, Bri, they wouldn't do that to you: it would be unethical, unprofessional and would place me in an invidious position. Better have a word with Jenny, though."

I asked Richard to put what he had said into writing. He declined. I asked if he would repeat what he said if asked to do so, he said he would.

Jenny Gaye advised me not to mention it: "Perhaps they won't notice." I really wanted the matter cleared up rather than possibly being paid the amount only to have it reclaimed at some date in the future. I received a memo from Jenny some days later confirming that Irene Chee had declared that from November, I would be paid 7.5 per cent CPF as were the old aunties (local cleaning ladies) lest, I suppose, I thought I was better than they were.

At break that day, I addressed the staff . . . loudly, telling them that they might like to know the kind of place they were working at, the kind of place that penalized people for becoming older and more experienced, who asked teachers such as me to face with equanimity the fact that they were earning considerably less than others in the staff-room simply because of their age. I had not noticed that a colleague was on the 'phone to Richard Allen at the time; he heard it all and panicked. He reported the incident to R. Errol Jaquierri who was School Superintendent, who reported it to Irene Chee, who said, "Sack him!"

Richard, God bless him, said, "No."

I did not find this out until some time later. You will be wondering how Richard could get away with gainsaying the village tyrant I describe. Richard was the first person to be employed by the School when it opened in 1991 with 39 students. The Chinese are very superstitious people and sacking the first employee is unlucky. Richard, as will emerge, was continuously being constructively dismissed, but refused to jump. He would never be pushed.

I went to ask Richard to come good on his promise:

"You do remember, Richard, saying, 'it would be unethical, unprofessional and would place me in an invidious position'?"

"No, I don't remember that."

"How very convenient."

"Are you saying that I have conveniently forgotten?"

"No. I am saying that it is convenient that you have forgotten."

End of interview and retirement plans. Whilst all this was taking place, other dastardly plots were afoot. Jenny Gaye was, evidently, locking horns with David Perry over academic policy involving her insistence on Heads of Department. She was getting way out of line. Errol Jaquierri was told to tell her that Irene Chee was in charge of the School not Jenny Gaye; Jenny would be the mouthpiece of Irene and David's wishes. Errol said, no, he could not convey such a message. He was sacked. I did not know this when a few days later, having presented my case to Irene and David and obviously having found out that I was for the chop, if not then, at contract renewal time, he took my hand and said, "I can get nowhere with your case. I just want to wish you all the best."

And he was crying, for God's sake! What manner of place was this?

Shortly after this, we were all called to an emergency staff meeting one break time to be confronted by a drawn Jenny Gaye.

"I want you all to know before the rumours start that I have just resigned. My position here is untenable."

And she walked out to a standing ovation, taking my Head of Department prospects with her. The Principal label was removed from her door and placed on the door of Richard Allen's office whilst Jenny was still serving out her notice.

In January 1995, Jenny opened her own school in Singapore, *Chatsworth*, with Heads of Department. I spoke to her shortly after the opening and, knowing the mind of Irene Chee, she said, "I cannot believe you are still there."

This was to become an oft-repeated phrase from those who knew the lie of the land. But there I stayed. I did make efforts to find a more secure environment but Jenny, my wife, now employed as a full-time ESOL teacher in the Elementary School, having acquired a Cambridge University TEFL Certificate, we could not immediately match our joint salary.

I weathered my first contract-renewal crisis by lowering my belly to the ground. Perry's answer to Jenny Gaye's insistence that the School could not function without departmental policies and guidance developed by professional heads of department was to initiate the scheme of Subject Area Leaders. These were to be responsible for co-ordinating departmental matters and reporting back ideas to the administration. In fact, they were used to report the edicts of the administration to the department. These roles were to circulate amongst the members of the departments on a termly basis, unpaid and without any kind of authority. You might have thought that such a scheme would die through lack of support such as I refused to grant it. But people were queuing up to do it as they could pass it off on their CV as Head of Department; people like Rob Sole, already referred to, who would never be *appointed* to such a role. My position was that it was a way of getting department donkey-work done not only on the cheap but very inefficiently and that we should have nothing to do with it. The first thing these SALs did has a familiar ring about it which I clearly heard in the distance when Perry first dreamed it up. It was to have the tenure extended to a year, then indefinitely subject to a majority vote in the department (which was readily given by those who did not want the non-job that had no effect on one's classroom experience anyway). It is now called Curriculum Area Leader (CAL) and is undertaken by people who are, by default, referred to as Heads of Department. The first such person in the English Department was Linda Lush a South African Woman with no teaching experience. She set about building an empire for herself and charmed her way into the pockets of the people she wrongly identified as having influence. Irene Chee did not like her and so her days were numbered. I received a letter from Richard Allen that came right out of the blue: I was uncooperative, not a team player, I inculcated a sense of failure in the classroom and so on. I showed it to Linda and asked if she knew anything about it. She confessed to being absolutely appalled and shocked by it. I went to see Richard and asked upon what he was basing such an attack, and told him how shocked Linda had been as she knew nothing about it.

"Linda said that she knew nothing about it?"

"Yes, it was a complete surprise to her."

"Brian, it *was* Linda Lush. It was all Linda Lush!"

I "*put in place strategies*," carried out questionnaires amongst the students, and generally HUMBLED myself in a most impressive manner. Linda, meanwhile, elicited a promise from R. Lee Webb, the Superintendent, to whom she had also reported my failings (thereby demonstrating her devotion to the school) that he would place her in a leadership role. Irene would have none of it. Linda had been cultivating Dick, the Head of English at UWC, setting up meetings ostensibly to learn how to run a department. On hearing of Irene's animus against her, she resigned "*with a heavy heart*" reporting that she had accepted a post at UWC. She was chosen by the kids to give the graduation homily and reduced Lee Webb to tears with her wisdom and sincerity. She spoke on responsibility which those in power have in a thinly veiled criticism of her own "shabby" treatment. She spoke of sexual responsibility, the graduands being hormonal teenagers in need of wise counsel. Shortly after, taking up her job at UWC Linda and Desmond Dick were caught workshopping one another in a broom cupboard. They were sacked. She left her husband and two kids one of whom is mentally handicapped. Desmond left his wife and three kids, and they were last heard of in Brunei.

After Jenny Gaye's resignation and Richard's promotion, a posse came riding into town led by Big Jim Bronger. *Yeehah!* Jim was from an American School in Egypt. He was to be School Superintendent and had his name carved from a piece of hickory wood on his Desk: Dr. JIM BRONGER. Big Jim brought his deputy with him: R. Lee Webb. They had a young tenderfoot in tow—R. Mike Martell—and a Californian called R. Dawn Clements who wore a very large gold lame bow in her hair. This was to initiate a most bizarre episode in the schools development:

"You ain't goin' a *believe* the changes, Brian."

Said Big Jim. He was right. He had done a recce of the place and in so doing had crossed swords with Irene Chee. During the summer vacation before his first term started, he had been sent home to America for a cooling-off period. He formed a plan of which I appeared to be part. He decided that a school worthy of the name should have a quality-produced literary magazine as well as the photographic year book that the School has. I was to be given two periods a week from teaching to develop this project.

"I wanna tell you, Brian, that they don't think much of you upstairs. The only reason you're here is that Richard refused to fire you. Now I don't know why it is: it could be anything: something a parent said: something someone spotted looking through your classroom window: something a kid said . . . who knows? But *hey,* I'm here to protect you from all that shit: as long as Jim Bronger's here, Brian Bishop's here."

Three months later, he was sacked. The official line was that he was returning to the States for health reasons.

"They've sacked you, haven't they, Jim?"

"Is the Pope a catholic?"

"A few weeks ago you said, 'as long as Jim Bronger's here, Brian Bishop's here.' They're not going to renew my contract are they?"

"If I were a betting man, I'd bet against it."

"Gee thanks, Jim."

"Hey, is this the kinda place in which you wanna hang out anyways?"

Lee Webb became Superintendent. Dawn Clements became Principal with Mike Martell as her Deputy. Richard Allen was moved into the newly created post of Dean of Students in which he spent the next four years without discovering what he was supposed to be doing. Richard seethed in private whilst upstairs played with him: he was the fly and they the "wanton boys." But Richard stuck it out—the fact that he was being paid about twice the amount of the rest of the staff helped. A colleague privy to board meetings told me "the way they talk to him is unbelievable."

"IB prepares people for university far better than "A" Level. After an IB Diploma course, university is a breeze. In English, for example, students study 8 texts at "A" Level and they study 15 in the same depth at IB."

I was teaching both courses and felt duty-bound to present the facts that really spoke for themselves: I have 8 periods a week to teach eight "A" Level Literature texts and 5 periods a week to teach fifteen IB texts. I will not insult your intelligence by claiming that we study the texts at the same depth. Both courses have virtues. They cater for different types of student. Briefly, I would say that "A" Level is like a bath whereas IB is a shower. Both can be invigorating.

The fallout was immediate. I should say, here, that I am an examiner for IB Language A1 Higher Paper 2, World Literature, and Theory of Knowledge and have the greatest respect for the programme. Prior to the meeting to which I refer, I had been to see Lee Webb to offer my opinion that it was inefficient to try to spread our resources across two programmes and that, in our situation the IB Programme should be the one we concentrated upon. I was, however, being asked to deliver both programmes and did not think there was any value in selling one short. An IB programme is as good as the school in which it is taught. Fifty per cent of the IB Language A1 (English Programme) is assessed outside of the examination room, 30 per cent in the school at which it is taught. The interpretation of "the spirit of the programme" will vary and with it the amount of help given to ostensibly "unaided work" and the level of challenge presented by the texts selected. Even the number of books actually taught can vary considerably according to interpretation. The level at which IB is taught, of course, is not necessarily determined by the level at which it is publicly examined.

Apart from "A" Level and IB there was also the OFS Graduation Certificate which was equivalent to an American High School Certificate requiring internal credits awarded by classroom teachers. This, of course relies entirely on the School's integrity. Lee told me, personally, that he thought that the OFS Graduation Certificate that he had to ratify was being compromised by the phoney credits being awarded, particularly in English. The Graduation Certificate was, therefore, in Lee's opinion, fraudulent and he thought that to maintain his integrity, he should resign. Just before this, Lee called me in for another dressing-down as his informers had been at him again, urging him to sort me out. I was unable to elicit from him just what it was that needed sorting out, nor would he name his informers. I report the amazing conversation.

"It's the impression I get from the jokes they make about you when we go for a drink together."

"Are you telling me that the fact that people make jokes about me is enough to condemn me?"

"I don't care if it's true: the perception is out there."

"Do you know what you've just said, Lee: you don't care if it's true? You lived through the McCarthy era, didn't you?"

"Yes, I did."

"And I presume that you are familiar with Arthur Miller's *The Crucible*?"

"Yes, I am."

"And yet you can still say that! You see, Lee, it's easy not to get in people's hair if you do not care about what you are doing. But if you care, if you are passionate about what you do, thinking it really does matter, you do, from time to time, get very frustrated when you are thwarted by stupidity."

I left. The last thing Lee said to me before he left was, "Keep passionate about what you do, Brian, a school needs passionate people."

I was very moved by his words and felt we had made a separate peace. Lee died of cancer shortly after.

Certainly there was considerable pressure to come up with grades that suited the administration. R. Hilary Richardson, an Art teacher and R. Daniel Toyne, an English teacher, were called to a meeting with Glenda Goering, the Kindergarten Principal and Irene Chee. Glenda's daughter, Abigail, had been awarded a "C" Grade by both Hilary and Daniel.

"My daughter is not a "C" Grade student. I'm not having it, Irene."

Glenda, you will gather, was a confidante. Hilary and Daniel would not relent. R. Steve Frost told me that he altered ("revised" was his word) the transcripts. On another occasion, days before Graduation, I witnessed one of the most shaming sights of my career. A student, who had a long record of idleness and disruptive behaviour, objected to the fact that he was not to graduate. He claimed, long after the event, that his English paper had not been marked properly as one of the papers he had handed in was missing, lost by us. This was clearly not the case. However, as his parents supported him, Steve Frost buckled rather than face the wrath of his masters who regarded parental dissatisfaction as a judgement of failure on the part of the staff. The student was allowed to rewrite the missing paper. Daniel was instructed to mark it and produce a mark that would then allow the student to graduate. I have seldom seen a more shamefaced teacher than Daniel presented as he sat in isolation, pen in hand, torn between saving his job by going along with what was clearly indefensible or sacrificing himself . . . for what? Had he refused, the paper would simply have been passed to another English teacher or anyone else capable of wielding a pen.

The reaction at the School to the events of September 11, 2001, was very revealing. I suppose my own response is best expressed in the words of a member of the Orthodox Christian Community in Singapore: "To take an aeroplane full of human beings and deliberately fly it into a building full of other human beings is an idea conceived of in the pit of hell."

We were all very firmly warned off consoling or counselling students showing signs of distress as we "were not trained to do so." What kind of sad commentary is that about the way we have compartmentalised ourselves? I, personally could not find composure until I had written the following poem for the school newsletter:

SEPTEMBER 11th 2001

From the dark hole, the void
The not-God
The Chaos come again

I hear

The silent Munchian scream The crying out of stones
The fatuous sunbeams' sighs

I smell

The stench of all Mankind
The fug of those who know
The rot within the brain

I taste

The foulness of decay
Corruptions bitter cud
Polluted springs and wells

I touch

The clammy hand of dread
The wounded side of Love
The splintered looking-glass

I see

A terrible beauty born
A flickering candlelight
A crooked finger raised

I had heard a New Zealand lady, brought up in the most idyllic natural surroundings that that beautiful country can offer, tell how her world was shattered one day when, as a child, she had stood on a chair to take down a book from a shelf in her father's study. It contained photographs of the Nazi extermination camps. She had no idea that human beings were capable of such atrocities.

"My world was changed forever."

I knew what she meant.

The idea of world changing events on a personal level does seem to involve a tussle with philosophy which most of us experience without it evolving into anything approaching to a "study" of philosophy. But this "tussle" can perhaps help us along our pathway of "understanding."

Hans-Georg Gadamer—February 1900–March 2002—was a German Philosopher. He challenged the idea so prevalent today that human beings are capable of arriving at objective truth. This was presented in his major work *Truth and Method*. The post-enlightenment error, Gadamer suggests is to draw a parallel between human thinking and the methodology of the Natural Sciences. The problem here is human beings. Our derived mental status will not allow this. Maybe I can allegorise this by writing of my experience with school librarians. Their often humorously expressed frustration of their tedious daily task was, "I could keep the library in some semblance of order it if were not for the students using it all the time!"

Gadamer suggests in *Truth and Method* that when I state, "I knew what she meant," I make a claim that requires clarification. Gadamer argues that we need help in understanding things from someone else's perspective. In order to do this we need to construct an idea or "conceptualize" it as he puts it. This results in producing an "horizon." This, of course, is what we do literally when we change the position in which we physically stand. We obtain a different view. "Prejudice" is, according to Gadamer a necessary part of this process.[8] We obviously come to this new idea as my friend did. With an already fixed idea. In her case was that human beings were not capable of such monstrosities. She, in fact, experienced an education. She was as I was on seeing the newspaper images of the liberation of Auschwitz, changed for ever. This is of vital importance, as our future behaviour will be based upon truth rather than fantasy.

I can recall as a young child waking up to see on the front page of *The News Chronicle* the pictures from the liberation of Auschwitz. One's happiness after seeing such images is never unalloyed. My parents, along with everyone else, were horrified.

A few weeks later it was my mother's birthday. I had been given a 10-shilling note for my birthday a week previously. With it I set out to buy a pair of leather gloves for my mother. I saw what I wanted in the window of a shop at the top of our road. This was Barking in the East End of London. The couple who served me seemed amused that this little boy was buying gloves for his mother telling them that 10 shillings was all he had. They gave me the gloves and as I was leaving the husband said "Ten and six!" His

8. Gadamer, *Truth and Method*, 247, 283.

wife thumped him and shouted "No!" The man was laughing, he clearly was not serious and thought it was a joke. My parents were delighted with the gloves and asked where I had bought them. When I told them they looked at each other giggling as if they had some secret. When I asked what the joke was, my mother whispered in a hushed and amused voice, "They're Jews!"

As recalled at the beginning, I went to school at Mile End, Cooper's Grammar school for boys, now in Dagenham. First day I was surrounded by a large, rowdy circle of boys who shouted, "Are you a Yid?" I did not know what a Yid was but quickly decided I did not want to be one and was released!

Later, I and two friends decided to visit Israel as guests of the Jewish Council on Kibbutz Amiad, in the Galilee, just below the Golan Heights. This was a life-changing experience.

We three are not Jewish but we regard the Holocaust as the most cataclysmic event ever to take place on planet Earth in that it imposes an almost impossible-to-meet challenge on the imaginative faculty of the human race.

In 1946 this was illustrated to Golda Meir by the British Governor's Chief Secretary: "Mrs. Meyerson, [her married name] you must agree that if the Nazis persecuted the Jews, [note the conditional statement] they must have had some reason for it."[9]

Human reason, even today, cannot cope with the fact that fellow human beings were seeking to exterminate all Jews on earth by rounding them up and gassing them. It is or was beyond our imaginations. That is what had to be changed to accept that, there are people who wish to kill Jews because they are Jews. This fact is not subject to rationalisation.

We three working guests on Kibbutz Amiad were arrogant rationalists of the type that is very common today. When we arrived at the Kibbutz, Adolf Eichmann who oversaw the deportation of much of the Jewish population to extermination camps where they were gassed had been tracked down and brought to Israel where the Supreme Court of Israel sentenced him to death by hanging. This was carried out whilst we were living on Kibbutz

9. Meir, *My Life*, 199.

Amiad. Shortly after this, a group of German students requested a visit to the Kibbutz in a gesture of friendship and reconciliation. This request had to be put to the Kibbutz membership.

We three guests were not part of this. Gerry who was a Jewish member of the Kibbutz was very similar to me except for this fact. He was of a similar age and, like me, came from the east end of London. We became friends. "Surely," we said, "the membership will agree; it is the way forward." "I expect so," replied Gerry. It was refused. We "oh deared" and "tutt tutted" as "knowalls" tend to do. Gerry calmly informed us. "Well you see, Jacob survived at Auschwitz when he was seven-years-old by agreeing to examine the corpses from the gas ovens and extract any gold teeth."

Miriam met the "angel of death" Dr. Mengele who experimented on her without anaesthetic, and she is unable to have children. These things were accompanied by the guttural German Language.

They are unable to hear it without severe psychological disturbance. They, like many others on the Kibbutz, had the tattoos on their arms as a constant reminder. I have never felt so small and insignificant in my life and swore then that I would never become involved in arguments about which I knew absolutely nothing.

It does seem to me that we have lost sight of the HUMBLING fact that we need assistance in solving or even in recognising our fundamental problems, as we cannot be objective in our thinking. We must accept the fact that it is ontologically impossible for us to be so. This requires HUMILITY that the trend of our development militates against.

In the 14th century Chaucer, an English poet, author, and Civil Servant, created the following character.

> A good man was ther of religioun,
> And was a povre PERSOUN of a toun;
> But riche he was of holy thoght and werk.
> He was also a lerned man, a clerk,
> That Cristes gospel trewely wolde preche;
> His parisshens devoutly wolde he teche.
> Benigne he was, and wonder diligent,

And in adversitee ful pacient;
And swich he was y-preved ofte sythes.
Ful looth were him to cursen for his tythes;
But rather wolde he yeven, out of doute,
Un-to his povre parisshens aboute
Of his offring, and eek of his substaunce.
He coude in litel thing han suffisaunce.
Wyd was his parisshe, and houses fer a-sonder,
But he ne lafte nat, for reyn ne thonder,
In siknes nor in meschief to visyte
The ferreste in his parisshe, moche and lyte,
Up-on his feet, and in his hand a staf.
This noble ensample to his sheep he yaf,
That first he wroghte, and afterward he taughte;
Out of the gospel he tho wordes caughte;
And this figure he added eek ther-to,
That if gold ruste, what shal yren do?
For if a preest be foul, on whom we truste,
No wonder is a lewed man to ruste;
And shame it is, if a preest take keep,
A [spotted] shepherde and a clene sheep.
Wel oghte a preest ensample for to yive,
By his clennesse, how that his sheep sholde live.
He sette nat his benefice to hyre,
And leet his sheep encombred in the myre,
And ran to London, un-to sëynt Poules,
To seken him a chaunterie for soules,
Or with a bretherhed to been withholde;
But dwelte at hoom, and kepte wel his folde,
So that the wolf ne made it nat miscarie;
He was a shepherde and no mercenarie.
And though he holy were, and vertuous,
He was to sinful man nat despitous,
Ne of his speche daungerous ne digne,
But in his teching discreet and benigne.
To drawen folk to heven by fairnesse
By good ensample, this was his bisynesse:
But it were any persone obstinat,
What so he were, of heigh or lowe estat,
Him wolde he snibben sharply for the nones.
A bettre preest, I trowe that nowher non is.

He wayted after no pompe and reverence,
Ne maked him a spyced conscience,
But Cristes lore, and his apostles twelve,
He taughte, but first he folwed it him-selve.[10]

This is my translation:

There was a town's parson. He was financially poor but in the way of thinking that directed his words he was very rich. He was academically intelligent but his learning was informed by the wisdom of the Christian gospel. It was his mission to pass the wisdom on to his parishioners by his words and behaviour. He was patient and understanding and very reluctant to punish any failures to strictly obey all the Church rules regarding financial contributions. He would rather pay parishioners' tithes himself than do that. He personally could manage on very little. His parish was very widespread yet whatever the weather he would visit by walking with the aid of a staff any parishioner troubled by sickness or other circumstances. The social rank of that parishioner was completely irrelevant to him. They were all God's children.

This personal example is what today we rather clumsily refer to as the "HIDDEN CURRICULUM." Our parson was much more down-to-earth and available than that. Relating to the family community over which he kept watch, he preferred to say: "It is a great shame to have a shitty shepherd and a clean sheep." Avoiding that shame he took to be a sacred duty. He did not, as some of his colleagues did, delegate this duty and escape to St. Paul's where he could be paid to pray for wealthy donors or maybe get a well-paid job as a guild's chaplain. He chose to stay "at home" and shepherd his sheep. But most of all, he was a HUMBLE man. He was courteous and kind and did not regard himself as a superior person. He was not scornful. He did not ridicule but led by example. However, if a parishioner of whatever social rank stubbornly refused to abandon their evil ways, he made them well aware of their misdoing. There was nowhere to be found a better priest. He did not concentrate upon a fastidious conscience nor pomp and ceremony

10. Chaucher, *Prologue*, lines 477–528.

but upon the teaching of Jesus and the twelve apostles which he followed and then taught others to do so.

When I arrived at Warwick University as a mature student in 1965 I was fortunate enough to be under the enormous influence of Professor G. K. Hunter[11] as a student of English and American Literature. Professor Hunter delivered an introductory General Lecture on the use of language. He was making a point on the compelling eloquence of simplicity that sometimes illuminates language at moments of extremity. He illustrated this with the address from the dock at the Sacco and Vanzetti trial.[12]

> This is what I say: I would not wish to a dog or to a snake, to the most low and misfortunate creature of the earth—I would not wish to any of them what I have had to suffer for things that I am not guilty of. But my conviction is that I have suffered for things I am guilty of. I am suffering because I am a radical and indeed I am a radical; I have suffered because I was an Italian, and indeed I am an Italian; I have suffered more for my family and for my beloved than for myself; but I am so convinced to be right that if you could execute me two times, and if I could be reborn two other times, I would live again to do what I have done already. I have finished. Thank you.[13]

"HUBRIS" in Greek Tragedy referred to Pride and a failure to acknowledge a reliance upon the gods. This led to "NEMESIS" or retribution. The goddess of retribution was "NEMESIS."

Following the scientific discoveries of what became known as "THE ENLIGHTENMENT" in the nineteenth century, Friedrich

11. Professor G. K. Hunter founded the Department of English and Comparative Literature Studies at Warwick University. He became Professor of English at Yale University and Chair of Renaissance Studies. He died in April 2008. He taught us the values and humanity conserved in great literature. Latterly, he thought that this was being wrecked by academic developments.

12. On August 23, 1977, Nicola Sacco, a shoe maker, and Bartolomeo Vanzetti, a fish seller, were the first to be executed by the electric chair. Many claimed that they did not receive a fair trial due to political bias and anti-immigrant sentiments.

13. Speakola, "Nicola Sacco and Bartolomeo Vanzetti." The quotation is from Vanzetti's statement.

Nietzsche declared "God is Dead"![14] This gave rise to "NIHILISM" ("NIHIL" is the Latin for "nothing"). This produced a crisis in human thought and in the HUMILITY that acknowledged our human requirement for behavioural guidance. With no god where was this guidance to be found?

Albert Camus liked to be known as an absurdist.[15] He believed that "reality" is irrational and meaningless. His philosophy was based upon what he regarded as the human limitation of "knowing the world." This clashed with his belief that a man without ethics is as a "wild beast" loosed upon the world.[16] But, he asks, what determines our human concept of right and wrong? Camus's first novel is *The Stranger* written when he was 22. The leading character, Meursault, is an Algerian. He kills an Arab for no apparent reason. Central to Camus' puzzlement is the question of the purpose of life: is life worth living? This, of course, is Hamlet's question in perhaps the most famous dramatic soliloquy ever written "To be or not to be?"

Camus could not accept any philosophy based upon the possibility of human beings, thinking objectively. Our thinking, Camus claimed, can only be based upon our individual SUBJECTIVE preferences and opinions. We can only conclude that life is absurd and purposeless. This is quite shockingly captured in *The Stranger*. With the weight of the evidence against Meursault in his murder trial is biased by the emphasis of the prosecuting lawyers upon his lack of emotional tears at his mother's funeral, Camus states, "In our society any man who does not weep at his mother's funeral runs the risk of being sentenced to death."[17]

In *Sisyphus*, Camus reflects upon the Greek myth where Sisyphus is punished for disobeying the gods by constantly pushing

14. Friedrich Wilhelm Nietzsche: October 1844–August 1900; German philosopher and leading modern thinker.

15. Albert Camus: November 1913, Algeria, to January 4, 1960, France. He was influenced by Nietzsche. He was a French Philosopher, author and dramatist. He was a political activist. In 1957 he received the Nobel Prize for Literature.

16. A phrase famously attributed to Camus.

17. Camus, preface to *The Stranger*, 19,

a boulder uphill that just as constantly falls back downhill requiring Sisyphus to try again. Camus views Sisyphus as a happy man. This constant rebellion, Camus concludes, is the meaning of our existence.[18] When being interviewed about his stage adaptation of Dostoevsky's *The Possessed* in 1959,[19] Camus identified that our human condition, as "the emptiness of the heart, the *impossibility* of holding to any faith or belief," was the reality we have to face.[20]

In the book of St. Matthew, chapter 18, of the Christian Bible, the disciples ask Jesus a question that perhaps demonstrates the competitive nature which still dominates us today: "Who is the greatest in the kingdom of heaven?" (verse 1).

We know exactly where we are here. Who is the best? We ask it all the time to our parents, to our school teachers; to our sports judges; to our choir judges etc. etc. etc. Jesus replies in a way that is very emotionally moving. Then, suddenly, we are brought up with an alarming start. "And Jesus called a little child unto him, and set him in the midst of them" (verse 2).

The child is, for Jesus, an example of unspoilt trusting innocence. We are surely at this point impelled to ask ourselves the rhetorical question, "What have we done?"

We have to accept that we have brought about a society where that image of childhood has been radically transformed to our utter shame.

> And Jesus called a little child unto him, and set him in the midst of them,
> And said, Verily I say unto you, Except ye be converted, and become as little children, ye shall not enter into the kingdom of heaven.
> Whosoever therefore shall *humble* himself as this little child, the same is greatest in the kingdom of heaven. (Matt 18:2–4; emphasis added)

In 1880, the Russian writer, Fyodor Mikhailovich Dostoevsky (1821–1881) published what Sigmund Freud claimed to be "the

18. Camus, *Myth of Sisyphus.*
19. Available on YouTube.
20. Ready, "Dostojewski on the Polish Stage"; emphasis added.

most magnificent novel ever written,"[21] *The Karamazov Brothers.* In 1849 Dostoevsky had been sentenced to death as a member of the Petrashevsky circle which was a group of utopian socialists. He was blindfolded on the scaffold awaiting execution when the word came through that his sentence had been commuted to exile. He was financially ruined by an obsession with gambling. These experiences transformed his personal ideology. As the publisher's note tells us *The Karamazov Brothers* explores "ideas about God, freedom, the collective nature of guilt, and the disastrous consequences of rationalism."[22]

The translator of the novel, Ignat Avsey, writes,

> *The Karamazov Brothers* ranges over an immensely wide spectrum of human concerns: family ties, the upbringing of children, the relationship between Church and State, and above all everyone's responsibility towards others. Zosima preaches collective expiation through the awareness of collective guilt; Dimitry, in the traditional Christian sense preaches collective expiation through the suffering of the innocent individual. The atheist Ivan is ready to see the disordered civic state subsumed under the authority of the church; the saintly Alyosha is ready to leave the certainty of the church for the turmoil of the world at large.[23]

Children, on whom a great deal of attention is lavished in the novel, are portrayed as enquiring, assertive individuals with a strong desire for an understanding of the world about them. In a characteristically immature manner they involve themselves amusingly in discussions such as "who founded Troy?," the meaning of socialism, and the role of the doctor in society. The spirit of enquiry is ever present.

In his novel, *Crime and Punishment*, Dostoevsky introduces Raskolnikov—a murderer—and Sonia—a prostitute. Two human beings who have reached the depths of degradation claim our

21. Freud, "Dostoevsky and Parricide," 177.
22. Dostoevsky, *Karamazov Brothers*, back cover.
23. Ignat Avsey, introduction to *The Karamazov Brothers*, xxiii.

attention. Sonia reads to Raskolnikov the whole passage from John's Gospel relating the story of Lazarus.

> "Then many of the Jews which came to Mary and had seen the things which Jesus did believed on Him." She could read no more, closed the book and got up from her chair quickly. "That is all about the raising of Lazarus," she whispered severely and abruptly, and turning away she stood motionless, not daring to raise her eyes to him. She still trembled feverishly. The candle-end was flickering out in the battered candlestick, dimly lighting up in the poverty-stricken room the murderer and the harlot who had so strangely been reading together the eternal book. Five minutes or more passed.[24]

It is a very tense and poignant scene within the context of the novel that deals with the theme of redemption. That which is inexplicable in post-enlightenment terms because it is not rational. Raskolnikov listening to this passage from the Bible and experiencing the atmosphere created by poor degraded Sonia is devastated. It is for us to come to terms about why this might be so.

Currently, we seem to look for wisdom to "culture gurus" whatever that means. One such is R. Ash Sarkar. She is described by Naomi Klein as "one of the boldest and most exciting thinkers of her generation."[25] Another view is presented by R. Will Lloyd in the "Culture Magazine" of the *Sunday Times*, 9th March 2025: "Ash Sarkar, a two-legged viral outrage generator beloved by television producers. . . . Screaming the word 'Nazi' at people, Sarkar was an inescapable presence of those high-pitched times."[26] Here is one of her latest thoughts: "Social media has partially but dramatically democratised the public sphere."[27]

Maybe you find that "most exciting" and I am missing something. But it does seem to me that the degraded prostitute possesses that which is lacking in one of the "boldest and most

24. Dostoevsky, *Crime and Punishment*, 439.

25. An endorsement given by Klein for Sarkar's *Minority Rule*.

26. Lloyd, "Ash Sarkar's Misadventures."

27. Sarkar, as quoted in Lloyd, "Ash Sarkar's Misadventures."

exciting thinkers of her generation." I am confronted with the Camus phrase "emptiness of the heart." This had been illustrated to me in 1970. I was teaching in the east of England. The headmaster of this school had been appointed when it was a Grammar school of 400 students. It was proposed that the school was to become a comprehensive school of 1,000 plus students. The headmaster was very opposed to this idea. He was obliged to attend a conference on the matter. On returning from this conference where it was made clear that it was government policy to convert all UK schools to the new comprehensive system, he gave the impression that he had in fact always supported the idea. He was a very religious man and very enthusiastic regarding morning assemblies where the whole school met for a brief religious service. The very well-known hymn of William Blake's poem "Jerusalem" was often selected to be sung but our headmaster (a Cambridge graduate) was concerned. As you will know, Blake's poem begins with the line: "And did those feet in ancient time / Walk upon Englands mountains green."[28] Our headmaster thought that we should alter this as children should be taught that it is grammatically incorrect to begin a sentence with a conjunction.

Thoughts bursting into words that it conveyed by the "And" is completely missed by "the emptiness of the heart" that Camus regards us as having inflicted upon ourselves and therefore our children. Remember that Sonia "could read no more. . . . 'That is all about the raising of Lazarus,' she whispered severely and abruptly, and turning away she stood motionless, not daring to raise her eyes to him."

St. Francis of Assisi is sometimes thought of as "God's Fool." There is a long history of "holy fools."

The "Holy Fool" functioned much as a Chorus would in Greek Tragedy. The purpose of the Chorus was to emphasize the moral themes and to clarify the inner development of what stage characters were performing and speaking. This gave a rounded performance that today is left to the skill of the writer, actors, and directors. The Chorus was prevalent in Greek Drama of the

28. Blake, "Jerusalem," stanza 1.

5th Century BCE. This function has developed in many ways over centuries. The "holy fool" had a long history in Russian Literature. It was a respected character although appearing as strange and even outrageous in what he performed or spoke. The main Character paid attention. The fools were licenced as the HUMILITY of the Great Man told him that what appears impertinence might be irrational wisdom.

Perhaps the most modern example of this phenomenon is Shakespeare's Fool in *King Lear*. In this Christian period of Western Europe the Biblical passage in 1 Corinthians 3, vv. 18 and 19, might have energised this development: "If any man among you seemeth to be wise in this world, let him become a fool, that he may be wise."

In act 1 scene 5 of Shakespeare's *King Lear* the fool challenges the King:

> Fool: If thou wert my Fool, nuncle, I'd have thee beaten for being old before thy time.
> Lear: How's that?
> Fool: Thou shouldst not have been old till thou hadst been wise.[29]

There is a universality about that statement for today's audience.

In 1966 R. Jan Kott published *Shakespeare Our Contemporary* where this idea is developed. Kott describes the fool as an individual whose responses are intuitive and far from foolish. His intuition succeeds where intellect fails. Good and evil are not presented as mental battles but battles of that, which we as a society have largely lost belief—the soul. I quote from Kott's book:

> [The Fool] does not follow any ideology. He rejects all appearances, of law, justice, moral order. . . . Lear, insisting on his fictitious majesty, seems ridiculous to him. . . . The Fool knows that the only true madness is to recognise this world as rational.[30]

29. Shakespeare, *King Lear*, act 1, scene 5, lines 40–44.
30. Kott, *Shakespeare Our Contemporary*, 132.

I suggest that perhaps we had our own "holy fool": this man, considered by contemporaries as mad, asked the stunningly child-like question of the "Tyger" whom he was addressing: "Did he who made the Lamb make thee?"[31] This, of course was William Blake who lived among us in 1757–1827. Those around him were becoming deliriously excited by the progress of the "industrial revolution," when the textile industry was the first to use modern production methods and textiles became the dominant industry in terms of employment and wealth. But our "holy fool" did not see this. What he saw was "dark satanic mills"[32] where children were treated cruelly and died unloved. But then, he was a fool and there are many lengthy and scholarly dissertations that present statistics and graphs to show that things were not as bad as all that. Only a fool would disagree with statistics and graphs after all!

Today, we have to suffer or be blessed, depending on our subjective opinion, by political leaders. Increasingly, fewer of us look to religious leaders for guidance. We are left with words and images to help us on our way.

In chapter 17 of St. John's Gospel we learn that Jesus is praying for his disciples. He says, "They are not of the world, even as I am not of the world" (verse 14). There is some confusion here because of language. This confusion is enlightened by St. Francis of Assisi where he is reported as saying, "Preach the gospel at all times and if necessary use words." St. Francis is surely referring to the vital importance of the HIDDEN CURRICULUM.

An image I cannot forget is of an occasion in 1962. I was on the Via Dolorosa in the old city of Jerusalem. This "sorrowful way" is the route Jesus took on his way to crucifixion. In the middle of the way stood a laden donkey. The donkey is the Grecian symbol of suffering and HUMILITY. The donkey's frustrated master was bearing his own weight against a wall with both hands behind him. He propelled himself forward and kicked the immobile donkey fully and violently in its stomach in an attempt to make it move forward. The creature remained immobile with that

31. Blake, "Tyger," stanza 5.

32. Blake, "Jerusalem," stanza 2.

beautifully serene face that donkeys bear. This is a very memorable HUMBLE image.

On Thursday, 9th January 2025, listening to the family eulogies to American President Jimmy Carter, we were moved by what we heard regarding a very great human being. I was reminded of Chaucer's Poor Parson. Of course there are many differences of detail. As mentioned in chapter 17 of St. John's Gospel in the Bible, Jesus praying says of his disciples that "they are not of the world, even as I am not of the world." Jimmy was very much more involved with "the world" than was Chaucer's parson. However, the remarkable thing about the man seems to have been his HUMILITY."

First and foremost he was a man of profound Christian faith. He seems to have regarded his work in the lowly role of a Sunday School teacher at least as vital as the highly elevated role as the President of the most powerful country of the Western World. And this led me to reflect on my academic work relating to Shakespeare's *Julius Caesar*. I had been asked to classify Shakespeare's Play: was it to be classed as a tragedy? I arrived at the understanding that the play was maybe not a tragedy in the classical definition as the "fall" of a socially elevated nobleman. But it did present the vision of a tragic world in which Cassius was likely to prove a better Emperor than Brutus. Reflecting on the fact that Jimmy Carter only survived as President for one term it seemed to me that we live in a tragic world where the populous (you and me) have decided that X (you decide) would make a better president than Jimmy Carter. Jimmy HUMBLY carried on with his role as Sunday School teacher for many years until his death at 100 years old. I am not saying that one has to be a Christian to cope with the guidance required in life. I simply put my thoughts forward and invite positive opposition from which I might learn.

At the age of 90, Jimmy published in his *A Full Life: Reflections at Ninety*. "I have tried, at least most of the time, . . . to acknowledge and try to correct my mistakes and weaknesses."[33] These are very memorable HUMBLE words from a man of profound faith.

33. Carter, *Full Life*, 97.

Camus came to the conclusion that "there is but one truly serious philosophical problem, and that is suicide. Judging whether life is or is not worth living amounts to answering the fundamental question of philosophy. All the rest . . . comes afterwards."[34] There is an inscrutable hiatus between what we fancy we know and what we really know. These are very memorable words from a man of no faith.

In the Republic of Venice, spiritual and charitable associations were referred to as *scuole,* that literally translates as "schools." In the rest of Italy the name for a comparable institution was a *confraternita* or a brotherhood. One of the most important tasks of such an association was the spiritual care of the dying and their burial, as well as general care for the poor.

There were a large number of local *Scuole piccolo* (small) and a few influential and wealthy *Scuole grandi. The Scuole Grande di San Rocco* dedicated to the plague-saint[35] had been formed in 1478 and was committed to charitable works on behalf of the poor and sick and it has survived to the present time. In 1564 it had moved to its current impressive premises. It is a large meetinghouse for the lay brothers of the *Scuola.* There was much local criticism at the time based upon the perception that the *Scuole* had lost sight of the HUMILITY upon the basis of which they had been formed. The poet Alessandro Caravia was particularly scathing. He was a neighbour of the painter Tintoretto in *sestiere Cannaregio* and a member of the *poligrafi.*[36]

Decisions based on wealth and social standing had developed and fragmented the various fraternities. Tintoretto's marriage to

34. Camus, *Myth of Sisyphus*, 3.

35. Saint Roch was invoked during various medieval plagues and because of the miracles attributed to his intercession he is labelled a patron against plagues.

36. *Poligrafi* was traditionally the term referred to a few versatile sixteenth-century intellectuals who were willing and able to write on any subject, hence the name: they were literary "hacks." It was applied to writers and publishers but expanded to describe a reformist network amongst the artisan community in Cannaregio. Printing became an explosive industry in sixteenth-century Venice undisturbed as it was by the wars of mainland Italy. It was three times less expensive to print in Venice than it was in Rome.

Faustina Episcopi with whom he had eight children sheds light upon the structure of Venetian society in the sixteenth century. Although not of the nobility, Faustina's family were high-ranking and members of the *cittadini originarli.*[37] These were those who could demonstrate three generations of Venetian descent and non-participation in artisan activity. To them alone positions in the Ducal Chancery were available and the self-interest of the *cittadini* confirmed them as staunch supporters of the oligarchic system rather than a potentially subversive element. Tintoretto's own social background is obscure. His father, Giovanni Battista Robusti, was a silk cloth dyer but whether or not he was financially involved in the production process or what his social standing was is unknown. Carlo Ridolfi was a painter and a biographer of artists. He wrote on Tintoretto. This contains anecdotal evidence of Tintoretto's personality and approach to life. The famous story illustrative of a certain class tension between Jacopo and Faustina regarding the Venetian toga that her status made available to him is amusing if of doubtful authenticity. Such stories, even if invented, tend to attach to a personality of which they seem illustrative. To that extent, at least, they have some value. We are encouraged to imagine Jacopo sulkily walking along the *Fondamenta dei Mori* in his toga as Faustina watches proudly from her window only for him to take it off and drag it through the mud on turning the corner.

Tintoretto was always a controversial man as well as a painter. He did not court popularity. But he was enormously important in his contribution to our "horizon."

At this stage, I strongly advise the reader to view the paintings of Tintoretto available on the website of *Scuola Grande di San Rocco* and in particular *Christ Washing the Disciple's Feet* (ca. 1547).

Tintoretto does seem to have been without the digressive business drive of the looming presence of Titian. Nichol's opening sentence to his 1999 study of Tintoretto is worth quoting at this point:

37. Original citizens.

> Jacopo Tintoretto was born and died in Venice. He is recorded away from his native city on only a single occasion (in September 1580, when he was briefly in Mantua) and the vast majority of his work was commissioned by Venetian patrons to adorn Venetian public buildings.[38]

Eloquent in its simplicity, this straightforward statement of fact seems to be of huge significance. This was not the way to "get on" in the Italian or European art world of the time. One has to assume that Tintoretto was not interested in "getting on" as the expression is usually understood. Titian[39] clearly was. The spirituality of Tintoretto's last signed work—*The Entombment of Christ* for "San Giorgio Maggiore" cannot be missed.

In fifteenth-century Venice there were more than two hundred *Scuole.*[40] They played a crucial role against poverty and other forms of distress. They were financed by a members' tax and bequests. Each *scuola* had a patron saint and a statute to which they were committed. There were six *Scuole Grandi*, large confraternities. The rest were *Scuole Piccole*, small confraternities. These smaller organisations tended to be based within local parishes. As they were parish based, these confraternities were smaller and more egalitarian in composition and far less wealthy than the *Scuole Grande.*

Tintoretto's controversial relationship with the *Scuole Grande* is well documented but he appears to have had an easier relationship with the guild and parish based *scuole.* By accepting commissions for parish-based *scuole*, Tintoretto would certainly have been aware of the humbler social circumstances of the membership to which he was addressing his paintings. It also seems to be that both Titian and Veronese painted one or, in the case of Veronese, maybe two works for such confraternities as opposed to thirty or more by Tintoretto. Clearly, Tintoretto's emphasis on the humble circumstances of the people to whom Jesus addressed his earthly

38. Nichols, *Tintoretto*, 13.

39. Titian: 1488–1576. The most important painter of the Venetian School.

40. The word *scuole* is the plural form of *scuola.*

ministry would have been attractive to such parish groups. There were, therefore, business incentives for populating his works with unsophisticated or comic characters. However, when looking at Tintoretto's painting for San Marcuolo—*Christ Washing His Disciples' Feet*—it is difficult to avoid the impression that he enjoys their company. The portrayal is full of good humour.

The de-emphasizing of the physical presentation of Christ is to be seen in Tintoretto's paintings, particularly noticeable in the cycle of paintings for *The Scuola Grande di San Rocco*. This adds to the sense of historical narrative although the setting is brought forward. Tintoretto makes no attempt to contextualize the event to its historical setting. The political situation of contemporary Venice with its empire and trading position with Asia and the colourful exoticism associated with it is very clearly evoked. The turbans and fezzes, a familiar daily sight for Tintoretto. There is no suggestion that these are anything but good honest people happy in each other's company.

Finally, it does seem that our human attempts to grow our understanding is more engaging than our politicians' attempts to grow our economic growth. On this human level past and present cannot exist without each other. Understanding, as Gadamer shows us, is always a "fusion of horizons."[41] The human faculty of imagination is crucial here and requires development that such artists as Tintoretto provide! The scope of imagination is described by Einstein as follows:

> Logic can take you from A to B, but imagination can take you everywhere.[42]

Gadamer points out that "the difference between methodological sterility and genuine understanding is imagination, that is the capacity to see what is questionable in the subject matter and to formulate [further] questions."[43] At the right time change of perspective might be possible by the employment of imagination.

41. Gadamer, *Truth and Method*, 317.

42. An expression attributed to Einstein.

43. Gadamer, *Philosophical Hermeneutics*, xi.

Nothing that needs interpretation can be understood at once. Wisdom can be gained or developed by experience. Our history and background must play a part in our present horizon and so contribute to a new one.

We must press on!

Bibliography

Bishop, Brian L. *Bug-Eyed Loonery*. New York: Samuel French, 2016.

Blake, William. "Jerusalem ['And Did Those Feet in Ancient Time']." 1810. Poetry Foundation. https://www.poetryfoundation.org/poems/54684/jerusalem-and-did-those-feet-in-ancient-time.

———. "The Tyger." 1794. Poets.org. https://poets.org/poem/tyger.

Camus, Albert. *The Myth of Sisyphus: And Other Essays*. Edited by Justin O'Brien. London: Vintage, 1983.

———. *The Stranger*. Edited by Harold Bloom. Philadelphia: Chelsea House, 2001.

Carter, Jimmy. *A Full Life: Reflections at Ninety*. New York: Simon & Schuster, 2016.

Chaucer, Geoffrey. *The Prologue: From the Canterbury Tales*. Edited by Richard Morris and Walter W. Skeat. Rev. ed. Oxford: Clarendon, 1889.

Dostoevsky, Fyodor. *Crime and Punishment*. Translated by Constance Garnett. London: Collector's Library, 2004.

———. *The Karamazov Brothers*. Translated by Ignat Avsey. Oxford: Oxford University Press, 1998.

Freud, Sigmund. "Dostoevsky and Parricide." In *The Standard Edition of the Complete Psychological Works of Sigmund Freud, Volume 21*, edited by James Strachey and Anna Freud, 173–96. London: Hogarth, 1961.

Gadamer, Hans-Georg. *Philosophical Hermeneutics*. Edited by David E. Linge. 2nd ed. Berkeley: University of California Press, 2004.

———. *Truth and Method*. Edited by Joel Weinsheimer and Donald G. Marshall. Rev. ed. New York: Bloomsbury, 2004.

Keats, John. "Hyperion." 1820. Poets.org. https://poets.org/poem/hyperion.

Kott, Jan. *Shakespeare Our Contemporary*. Translated by Boleslaw Taborski. London: Methuen, 1967.

Lazarus, Emma. "The New Colossus." 1883. Poets.org. https://poets.org/poem/new-colossus.

Lloyd, Will. "Ask Sarkar's Misadventures in the Culture War." *The Times*, Feb. 27, 2025. https://www.thetimes.com/culture/books/article/minority-rule-adventures-culture-war-ash-sarkar-review-jo3cxsco7?gaa_at=eafs&gaa_n=AWEtsqfM5pahmq3cOQBMzWmPIQUWzI9BkT4WbvZadWBmV9H4ntNanmdL4EgaYSZoeoA%3D&gaa_ts=69a06bd6&gaa_sig=-8TcgcSfkdQ7WMVvWeWXWZc4XscdGc2m4pauB3eJLcC-tGAttl4j1Ko1BeV-98swvaZUJi1rCZKNwgtm947htw%3D%3D.

Meir, Golda. *My Life*. New York: Putnam's Sons, 1975.

Nichols, Tom. *Tintoretto: Tradition and Identity*. London: Reaktion, 1999.

Okoth, Brian. "Lee Kuan Yew: Prime Minister Who Told Striking Pilots, 'I'll Teach You a Lesson You Won't Forget.'" Standard, Nov. 5, 2022. https://www.standardmedia.co.ke/article/2001459910/prime-minister-who-told-striking-pilots-ill-teach-you-a-lesson-you-wont-forget.

O'Neill, Onora: *A Question of Trust: The BBC Reith Lectures 2002*. Cambridge: Cambridge University Press, 2002.

Ready, Oliver. "Dostojewski on the Polish Stage." Times Literary Supplement. https://www.the-tls.com/arts/theatre/dostojewski-on-the-polish-stage.

Shakespeare, William. *Hamlet*. Folger Shakespeare Library. https://www.folger.edu/explore/shakespeares-works/hamlet/read/.

———. *King Lear*. Folger Shakespeare Library. https://www.folger.edu/explore/shakespeares-works/king-lear/read/.

Speakola. "Nicola Sacco and Bartolomeo Vanzetti: 'I Am Never Be Guilty, Never!', Pre Execution Statements—1927." https://speakola.com/ideas/sacco-vanzetti-execution-courtroom-1927.

www.ingramcontent.com/pod-product-compliance
Lightning Source LLC
LaVergne TN
LVHW020659100826
845148LV00012B/2564

* 9 7 9 8 3 8 5 2 6 6 9 7 5 *